#startupeverywhere

Startup Guide Johannesburg

EDITORIAL
Publisher: **Sissel Hansen**
Editor: **Marissa van Uden**
Proofreaders: **Ted Hermann, Shelley Pascual**
Staff Writers: **Charmaine Li, L. Isaac Simon**
Writer: **Tom Jackson**
Contributing Writers: **Kevin Hanley, Adam Oxford**

PRODUCTION
Global Production Lead: **Eglė Duleckytė**
Local Project Manager: **Asanda Kaka**
Researchers: **Vera Oliveira, Sofia Silva, Kendal Makgamathe, Gerald Masuku**

DESIGN & PHOTOGRAPHY
Designer: **Daniela Castanheira**
Photographers: **Moon Mokgoro, Earl Abrahams**

Additional photography by Blowfish Productions, WeThinkCode_, Wits Business School, UJ Comms and Unsplash.com

Illustrations by **Joana Carvalho, Cat Serafim, Daniela Castanheira**
Photo Editor: **Daniela Carducci**

SALES & DISTRIBUTION
Global Partnerships Lead: **Marlene do Vale marlene@startupguide.com**
Startup Ecosystems Manager: **Logan Ouellette logan@startupguide.com**
Business Developer - APAC and Africa: **Anna Weissensteiner anna@startupguide.com**
Marketing and Distribution: **Vera Oliveira vera@startupguide.com**

Printed in Berlin, Germany by
Medialis-Offsetdruck GmbH
Heidelbergerstraße 65, 12435 Berlin

Published by **Startup Guide World ApS**
Kanonbådsvej 2, 1437 Copenhagen K

info@startupguide.com
Visit us: **startupguide.com**
@StartupGuideHQ

Worldwide distribution by Die Gestalten
Visit: gestalten.com

ISBN: 978-3-947624-17-1

STARTUP GUIDE
JOHANNESBURG

STARTUP GUIDE JOHANNESBURG

In partnership with Tshimologong Precinct

Proudly Powered by

Supported by

Sissel Hansen
/ Startup Guide

Johannesburg – often known as Joburg or Jozi – emerged as a result of the gold rush in 1886 and has long been known as an international center for finance and trade. Nowadays, the ever-evolving city is seeing a community full of techies sprout up all over the city and it's building up its reputation as a startup hub. With a diverse population, vibrant cultural scene and bustling business landscape, Johannesburg is poised to become one of Africa's most disruptive ecosystems.

South Africa's largest city boasts a number of accelerator and incubator programs for budding startups across many different industries, with players that include the JamLab accelerator program for journalism and media innovators, AlphaCode Incubate for fintech ventures, and J&B Hive accelerator for creative entrepreneurs, to name a few. Additionally, Johannesburg's history as a business hub means that there are many corporates sprinkled across the city that startups can reach out to and potentially partner up with.

Although there are a few areas that need to be improved in order for the startup scene to reach the next level – such as gaining access to later-stage investment, strengthening the transportation infrastructure around the city and bridging the talent gap – the future looks bright, and there's an exciting crop of startups striving to use their business as a vehicle for social change. For instance, BrownSense Group is transforming the way that Black-owned South African businesses grow by connecting its community members directly with their target consumers. And then there's HomeFarm, a smart food-growing platform that helps users grow healthy food in the comfort of their own home.

We can't wait for you to get a look inside some of Johannesburg's most exciting startups, founders, investors, schools and accelerators, and we can't wait to share with the world what the city's innovators have to offer.

Sissel Hansen
Founder and CEO of Startup Guide

Local Community Partner / Tshimologong Precinct

Johannesburg is based within a vibrant South African entrepreneurial ecosystem. There is an abundance of incubators and coworking spaces, award-based pitching sessions, tax rebates and compliance driven by policy to incentivize corporates to invest in startups.

With the city having been built on the gold rush of 1886 and still maintaining that entrepreneurial spirit, it has both the highest concentration of high-net-worth individuals on the African continent and a leading economic engine. As the entrepreneurial ecosystem matures, so too are we collaborating to support startups across the value chain of their venture's lifecycle.

Tshimologong Precinct is a digital-innovation district founded by Wits University in 2016. Our mission is to realize African digital innovation for global markets. We collaborate with academia, corporates, provincial government and international development agencies to grow the talent pipeline of the digital economy by developing entrepreneurial digital skills. We exploit the conditions of thriving innovation ecosystems: we're close to research universities, within an existing business area, have a fantastic infrastructure and great wifi connectivity, and we're based in a neighborhood with a lifestyle of work, live and play.

We are home to international tech corporates, such as IBM's Research Lab and Siemens. We also host and support homegrown tech ventures, such as Raphta, Technovera and Smart City working in IoT, robotics and AI. Tshimologong Precinct's offerings include a range of incubation and accelerator programs for digital entrepreneurs, a Digital Skills Academy that converts unemployed youth to sought-after talent, an Animation Development Studio that specializes in the Africanization of imagery and storytelling, and a MakerSpace for rapid prototyping in fabrication. Join us for the annual Faku'gesi Festival, a ten-day festival bringing together innovators at the crossroads of arts, culture and technology.

Johannesburg is a city rich in diverse culture and opportunity. Although the city is developed, it is relatively new compared to major global markets, so there is room for startups to take part in shaping its future. Your imagination, energy and talent are welcome!

Lesley Donna Williams
CEO

contents

STARTUP
GUIDE
JOHANNESBURG

Local Ecosystem

[Facts & Figures]

- The City of Johannesburg is South Africa's economic heart. It is home to the Johannesburg stock exchange and is the national and continental headquarters for many global tech companies, law firms and banks.
- The local currency is the rand (ZAR).
- National languages spoken are Afrikaans, English, isiNdebele, Sepedi, Sesotho, Siswati, Setswana, Xitsonga, Tshivenda, isiXhosa and isiZulu.
- There are more than 220 programs offering support to startups and entrepreneurs based in Johannesburg.
- Around 30% of startups in Johannesburg are fintechs.
- Gauteng province, which covers Johannesburg and the nation's administrative capital, Tshwane, would be the seventh largest economy in Africa were it a country.
- The tallest building in Africa is the Carlton Centre in downtown Johannesburg, at 223 meters. Johannesburg is also home to the third tallest building on the continent, Ponte City. Both will be eclipsed by The Leonardo in Sandton when it is finished this year.
- Eighty percent of startups in Johannesburg say they have no problem with access to customers.
- There are between 350 and 450 tech startups in Johannesburg.

[Notable Startups]

- Internet of things specialist IoT.nxt raised more than 100 million ZAR ($7 million) in private equity in 2017.
- Stokfella, a fintech that modernizes *stokvels* (informal savings cooperatives), raised 1 million ZAR ($70,000) in seed funding in 2018.
- i-Pay, an electronic funds transfer (EFT) payment gateway, received 10 million ZAR ($700,000) in funding last year from VC firm Kanlon.
- Recent exits include parcel-delivery app Wumdrop, which was acquired by local retailer Massmart for an undisclosed amount.

Sources: City of Johannesburg (**wazimap.co.za**); Council on Tall Buildings and Urban Habitats (**ctbuh.org**); "Evaluation and Network Analysis of the Johannesburg Tech Sector Report" (2018 report by Endeavour Insight); "Gauteng Entrepreneurial Ecosystem Snapshot" by ANDE (**ecosystems.andeglobal.org/snapshot/gauteng/2018**); Statistic South Africa (**www.statssa.gov.za**); Ventureburn (**ventureburn.com**).

[City] Johannesburg, South Africa

GDP: ~$5 billion
Land area: 1,648 km^2
Population: 4.95 million
Population Density: 3,002.2 per km^2
Population of Greater Johannesburg
Area: 11 million

STARTUP GUIDE JOHANNESBURG

Aerial View - City of Johannesburg Metropolitan Municipality, Johannesburg

Intro to the City

In South Africa, Cape Town has the beaches and big VC community, and Tshwane is home to the civil service; but if it's the people, money and a truly international city you're after, you go to Johannesburg.

The city goes by many names: locals call it "Jozi" or "Joburg," while tourist guides call it the "City of Gold" because it sits on the world's largest known gold deposit. That drew settlers in the nineteenth century, and it has always been a city built on migration. Today, around 25 percent of the inner-city population was born overseas.

Johannesburg has a reputation for being dangerous and uninviting, and visitors are more likely to head to South Africa's coastline or game parks than to the economic capital; but dare to scratch its surface, and you'll find a cosmopolitan city with friendly people, a rich nightlife and a tech community that rivals any in the world. The two main central business districts are being transformed as new buildings go up almost daily. Hardcore tech entrepreneurs will make their way to downtown Braamfontein, where IBM's African Research Lab sits next to the Tshimologong Precinct, a university-sponsored coworking space, while the more genteel will gravitate towards the fintech hubs clustered around Sandton's banks.

Like the rest of the country, Johannesburg is marked by incredible inequality, and the mansions of the rich northern suburbs are hard to reconcile with the shacks and townships of the sprawl. But for the entrepreneur who sees problems as an opportunity to build solutions, the city is bubbling with potential.

Before You Come

It's best to sort out somewhere to stay and learn a bit about the different areas of the city before you arrive in Johannesburg. Crime isn't quite as rampant as many make out, but there are definitely places to avoid, at least on your first few days. It's best not to get lost without a local guide to help out. Plus, the speed of business can seem glacial to foreigners, and renting property can take time to sort out. Do be prepared for a lot of paperwork and seemingly invasive bureaucracy. Passport and cellphone numbers will be recorded at almost every building entrance and at many non-public parking lots. Don't worry too much about bringing a lot of cash, as almost everywhere takes card payments. However, a pocketful of change is essential for tipping informal workers, like the people who keep an eye on your car while you go shopping.

Cost of Living

Johannesburg is not an overly cheap place to set up shop compared to other African cities, although it does offer a little better value than New York or London. At the supermarket, you can expect to pay 77 ZAR/kg ($2.50/lb) for a packet of chicken breasts, for example, and a block of cheddar cheese is 132 ZAR/kg ($0.26/oz). Housing prices are generally good value for money too, and a two-bedroom apartment in a good part of town should cost around 8,000 ZAR ($560) per month. When you include essentials such as insurance, internet costs and medical aid, things can quickly get expensive. Transport is especially costly, and you'll find it tough to find anywhere to live within walking distance of your work. Eating and drinking out is pleasantly affordable, and you can get a great meal for less than 140 ZAR ($9.80).

Cultural Differences

Johannesburg is home to so many different cultures, it's hard to pinpoint one set of things to watch for. It's a true melting pot, with people from all over the country and continent everywhere. The good news is that it's also difficult to make an accidental faux pas. Few topics are off limits, it's hard to give offence, and Joburgers' willingness to engage in difficult subjects can be disconcerting to some.

Unlike most countries, South Africa has five seasons: spring, summer, autumn, winter and "strike." Annual wage disputes are often interspersed with service-delivery protests over poor infrastructure. One thing to be aware of is that manual labor in South Africa is cheap and unemployment is high, so jobs that may seem archaic to foreigners still exist here. For example, it may surprise some visitors when they aren't allowed to fill their own cars at a gas station and supermarket checkouts still have bag packers.

Commissioner Street - Johannesburg

Rain in a skyscraper core - Ponte City Tower, Johannesburg

Renting an Apartment

Renting as a foreigner can be tricky if you don't have proof of income or residency. Many rentals are also in "complexes" or small gated communities that will have private security and rules around noise and communal areas. There are a lot of new apartment spaces being built, which is helping to keep prices down, but the closer you are to the major startup hubs, the more you can expect to pay. Like any major city, rent prices range from affordable to absurd, and properties on the lower end of the scale can be more than a little "edgy." You can expect charges to go up by an arbitrary 10 percent every year, too, if you stay that long. On the other hand, it's common for rents to cover local taxes and sometimes utilities too. Note that private landlords will often require two and a half months rent in advance, plus a services deposit and a commission for the agent.

See **Flats and Rentals** page **190**

Insurance

South Africa has a public health system, and emergency services are theoretically free at the point of use for all. However, lines at public clinics can be extremely long, and if you're not there early, you may not be seen at all. Worse, it's hard to know what services you're supposed to pay for, and foreigners are often charged for services that should be free. The private health network, on the other hand, is both extensive and easily accessible. Basic GP visits in the private sector cost from around 400 ZAR ($30), and hospital treatments are usually much cheaper than overseas. There's little consistency in costs between providers, however, and the process of getting a referral to a specialist can be complex for those used to a more integrated system. Most local medical schemes will offer coverage for foreigners if you have a South African bank account. Note that even with insurance, you can expect to pay a surcharge for many out-of-hospital expenses.

See **Insurance Companies** page **191**

Nelson Mandela Bridge - Park Station, Johannesburg

Visas and Work Permits

Bureaucracy in South Africa is, frankly, horrendous, especially for foreigners. Every government office has its own interpretation of official rules and regulations, and you'll need to make multiple certified copies of every important document you have before applying for anything. This involves going to a police station and asking the desk officer to stamp, date and sign at least three copies of your passport, driver's licence, proof of address and anything else that's been requested. It's recommended to always get more copies than the requirements stipulate and copy more documents than you've been asked for. Always be prepared for long lines and long wait times. If you find it difficult to get the required paperwork organized in your country (many processes call for a police clearance certificate, for example, or signed affidavits), be warned that saying, "My country doesn't issue those" will not get you a pass.

Work visas can be acquired in several ways: employers can assist with a special skills permit, spouses of South Africans can apply for a special work visa, and entrepreneurs can apply for a temporary residence "business visa." Business visas usually have a capital requirement, which is reduced for certain priority industries. Although ultimate responsibility for visas lies with the Department of Home Affairs, in most cases the entire process is outsourced to VFS Global, whose Johannesburg office is in Rivonia, to the north of Sandton.

See **Important Government Offices** page **190**

Taxes

With few exceptions, if you earn money in South Africa, you must register to pay taxes there, and you're taxed on global income. Registering isn't difficult, as long as you have a work permit, but you'll need to physically visit the SARS office to do so. SARS prefers directors of companies to pay taxes monthly as an employee, although it is possible to pay every six months as a provisional taxpayer. There are no particular tax incentives for entrepreneurs, though: company dividends are taxed at the usual rate. VC funds, however, do get the benefit of "Section 12J" tax reductions. Although employee taxes are collected monthly, most taxpayers must file an annual return that includes details of assets owned in South Africa and overseas. It's advisable (though not essential) to use an accountant. As SARS isn't yet fully modernized, you can't file taxes directly via external software, and many accountants still use manual processes.

See **Accountants** page **190**

University of the Witwatersrand - Johannesburg

Starting a Company

The most common form of limited liability company in South Africa is the proprietary company or PTY. Sole traders can operate without formally registering a company, but they will be unable to open a business bank account or employ staff, and they will need to report company income on their personal tax return. Registering a company means filing forms with the Companies and Intellectual Properties Commission (CIPC). All of this can be done online and costs up to 475 ZAR ($33). Registration should be confirmed within three to five days. It's a pain-free process, as long as you have the right visas, of course.

There are plenty of cost-effective legal services available should you need to draw up partnership agreements with a cofounder, and most startup hubs will have advisors on hand too. Separate registrations need to be made with the South African Venue Service (SARS) for VAT and employment taxes. Applying for these is also simple but can take up to three months. Watch out for VAT: technically you can't charge VAT until you have a VAT number, but SARS may backdate the certificate and expect you to pay the VAT you would have been charged on old invoices.

See **Programs** page **53**

Opening a Bank Account

Visitors to South Africa are often surprised by the level of innovation in its banking system: automated cellphone banking has been a standard offering here for nearly twenty years and predates the birth of the smartphone. Locals can open a bank account with FNB just by sending a selfie on their smartphone, as the bank has access to the Home Affairs biometric database. As a foreigner, you'll need copies of your passport, proof of residence or visa and usually a payslip or letter from an employer. Monthly fees on accounts can range from between 50 ZAR ($3.50) to more than 200 ZAR ($14), so shop around before signing up. ATM withdrawal fees are from 6 ZAR ($0.40) to 8 ZAR ($0.60), or more if you use another bank's machines. The five main banks are FNB, Standard Bank, ABSA, Nedbank and Capitec. Beware if you plan to transfer money out of the country, as there are strict capital exchange controls in place.

See **Banks** page **190**

Dancing in the street - Johannesburg

Getting Around

Joburg's roads aren't as congested as Cape Town's or Nairobi's, but they have a well-earned reputation for being dangerous. Speed limits are rarely observed, and many drivers are unlicensed and road rules are poorly enforced, as traffic cops are notoriously open to bribes. Also, watch out for potholes. Many locals commute using the minibus taxi network, but it's not advisable for newcomers to try them out without a guide. They're cheap, but routes aren't always fixed, vehicles are often unsafe and drivers are known for being reckless. There are several bus companies, but they aren't especially reliable and stops aren't always convenient. The Gautrain rail network, on the other hand, is a good way of moving between Sandton, downtown, Rosebank and the airport, and there are plans to expand the service soon. Fortunately, there's plenty of choice when it comes to cab-hailing apps, and prices for these are reasonable. It's recommended that you start with these.

Phone and Internet

South Africa has strict laws around purchasing mobile SIM cards, and you'll need to produce proof of ID and residence in order to get one. It's best to pick up a local SIM at the airport, where the process is generally quicker. There are four main cell networks: MTN, Vodacom, Cell C and Telkom. Vodacom and MTN trade on the size of their network, but the smaller operators compete on price. Cell C, for example, offers free data for topping up airtime on pay-as-you-go, while Telkom's FreeMe data packages are the best overall value for money for mobile internet on contract, at 305 ZAR ($21) for 5 GB per month. For the most part, however, mobile or fixed line internet is expensive in South Africa, and data bundles currently expire after thirty days. Fiber options are widely available to the premises in Johannesburg, with excellent speed and reliability. Expect a 50 Mbps line to cost around 1,000 ZAR ($70) a month.

Commissioner St - Johannesburg

Learning the Language

There are eleven official languages in South Africa, and isiZulu is the most widely spoken in the homes of Joburg residents. The mix of cultures and languages means that many locals speak a colorful vernacular when among friends, which combines words from multiple languages. Generally speaking, though, English is the universal lingua franca in Joburg and also the predominant language of government and business. If you do want to brush up on your greetings before arrival, *sawubona* or *unjani* are isiZulu for "hello," although *heita* (which has its roots in isiXhosa) is also commonly used. You'll inevitably be invited to a *braai* at some stage, the Afrikaans word for barbeque. It's easy for newcomers to be thrown by people's names, as many common South African first names are gender neutral and have multiple spellings depending on the person's home language. South African English is delightfully quirky, however: for example, traffic lights are called "robots," much to the delight of geeks everywhere.

See **Language Schools** page **191**

Meeting People

For many Joburgers, leisure time means the braai and you'll likely receive plenty of invitations to meet people over a long lunch at the houses of colleagues or fellow entrepreneurs. For conversation, South Africans are crazy about sports, and Joburgers are no exception. Soccer is huge and while the local derby between the Orlando Pirates and Kaizer Chiefs will bring Soweto to a halt, European leagues are more popular than the local ones. Rugby and cricket, too, are widely adored and there are regular international matches at the local venues Ellis Park and The Wanderers.

All the startup hubs have regular networking events, including Impact Hub's monthly F-Up Night, where you can celebrate the value of failure. For something more hands on, try makerspace House4Hack in nearby Centurion, which has open evenings every Tuesday. The city also has world-class jazz clubs, such as The Orbit in Braamfontein, and plenty of theatres and restaurants. Joburg is also surrounded by amazing national parks, such as Pilansberg, for a weekend away.

See **Spaces** page **75**

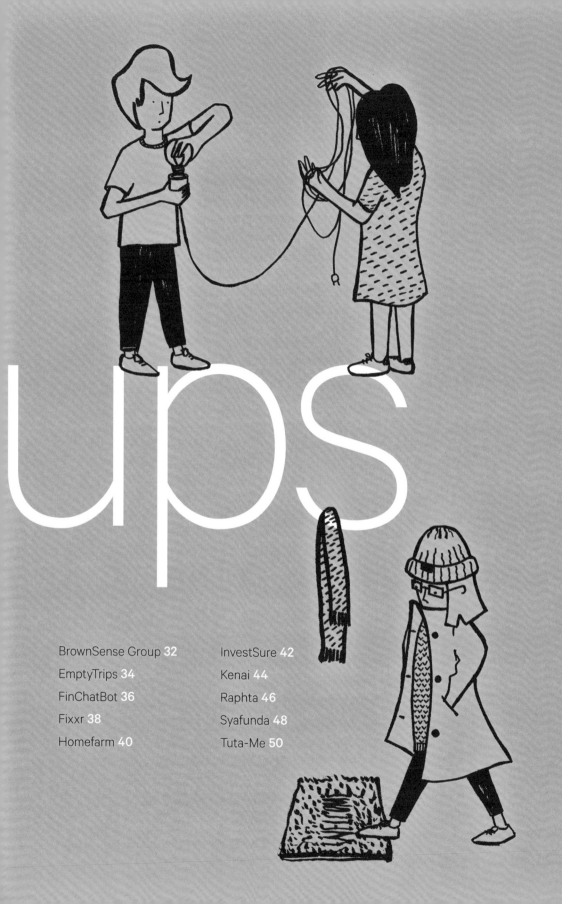

ups

[Name] # BrownSense Group

[Elevator Pitch] *"We're a platform that provides Black-owned businesses with access to markets, primarily through a 177,000-member Facebook group in which people can procure and market goods and services."*

[The Story] BrownSense Group was founded in 2016 for the sole purpose of helping Black-owned South African businesses gain access to markets, with or without funding. Since then, the bootstrapped business has grown organically and built a community of more than 177,000 people on its Facebook group, all trading together and helping businesses grow. "It came about as a result of seeking solutions that would be driven by the people and not by corporate or government," says founder Mzuzukile Soni. The startup now does everything from hosting monthly flea markets to undertaking research for big business and governments, providing procurement services and training entrepreneurs.

BrownSense Group partnered with The Hookup Dinner, Paybook and Tsoga Afrika to launch The People's Fund crowdfunding platform in 2017, and it also rolled out The People's Stokvel (an investment society) to help people invest. The BrownSense Foundation helps underprivileged individuals with disaster relief. The company is achieving lasting impact in South Africa, and Mzuzukile is optimistic about its potential for helping people even further afield and in different ways. "We have enabled people to leave their eight-to-five jobs to be full-time business people," he says. "We have started work on building an ecommerce platform. The long-term plan includes branching off into the continent to facilitate transactions amongst Africans within the continent and in the diaspora."

[Funding History]

Bootstrap

BrownSense has been entirely bootstrapped and self-funded since its launch, with the business scaling using its own revenues.

[Milestones]
- Launching The People's Fund, which has helped small businesses raised over 1 million ZAR ($70,000) so far.
- Rolling out The People's Stokvel, which has participating members contributing 100 ZAR ($7) per month.
- Launching the BrownSense Foundation, which has played an instrumental role in disaster-relief initiatives.
- Securing the Centre for Competition Regulation and Economic Development (CCRED) as our research partner.

[Links] Web: **brownsensemarkets.co.za** Facebook: **brownsensesa** Twitter: **@brownsense**

[Name]
EmptyTrips

[Elevator Pitch]
"We power an intermodal freight open exchange that instantly matches carriers and shippers to book, auction, manage, store and insure freight."

[The Story]
In Benji Coetzee's previous life as a management consultant, difficulties associated with moving products were recurring issues for clients. Businesses were often overcharged, even when carriers regularly had empty space. She resolved to reduce this damaging mismatch using a scalable, data-driven approach; thus, EmptyTrips was born. The startup developed an open marketplace that uses smart algorithms to match supply and demand of cargo transport, bringing transparency to the sector via its anonymous online bidding portal. "I compare our matching algorithms to those of dating sites, finding a possible match with some degree of success across large samples, but it is for freight and space," says Benji.

After testing with a few partner companies, Benji decided to make EmptyTrips available to everyone and quit her job to focus on it full time, officially launching in 2017. The portal now boasts an independent, asset-less fleet of more than six thousand trucks, and has registered more than 250 cargo shippers and offered more than two thousand trips. In 2018, EmptyTrips launched RailFOX, allowing companies to book, quote and bid for freight space on rail services among South Africa, Zambia and Zimbabwe. "Rail as a white-space opportunity truly was based on a gut feeling and has been quite an endeavor," says Benji. EmptyTrips has strategically partnered to roll out RailFOX in the US and Brazil, focusing on commodities with high payloads.

[Funding History]

Seed

EmptyTrips closed a multi-million rand funding round in 2017 from Unicorn Capital Partners. Currently, it is self-funded, with the startup focused on scaling using only its own revenues.

[Milestones]
- Launching our prototype into the market in 2017.
- Finally securing seed funding.
- Winning a host of awards, including the Singularity Ventures 2018, South Africa Innovation 2017 and IITPSA Technology Excellence award 2018.
- Pivoting into rail, which had a significant influence on the business, people and technology strategy.

[Links]   Web: emptytrips.com Twitter: @EmptyTrips Instagram: emptytrips

FinChatBot

[Name]

[Elevator Pitch]

"We develop bespoke AI-powered chatbots to help financial-service providers acquire and retain customers while reducing operating costs. Our smart chatbots enable clients to customize and automate important customer interactions, including quotes, sales conversions, debt collection, customer service and claims."

[The Story]

Founded in 2017, FinChatBot uses the latest artificial intelligence technology to help financial-service providers acquire and retain customers while reducing operating costs. Its smart chatbots enable the customization and automation of important customer interactions. It was launched by French entrepreneurs Antoine Paillusseau and Romain Diaz after they recognized that call centers were becoming increasingly inefficient, saturated and expensive, often not delivering the intended results of conversion and customer satisfaction. "We dedicated FinChatBot to the goal of bringing people closer to financial services with an interactive and fun experience while enabling financial-service providers to enhance customer experience and maximize business performance," said Antoine.

FinChatBot is able to deploy chatbots on multiple platforms, including client websites and messaging platforms. Its chatbots, enriched with machine learning, offer a more intuitive and efficient customer journey. On the back of its second funding round, which was secured recently, it expanded its team to ten people and has signed major clients, including Fedgroup and Bidvest Insurance. Its current strategy is to focus primarily on the financial industry and cement its foothold in the South African market, but it already has had requests from companies in other industries and other African countries, as well as from Europe and the US. "Our flexible and tailor-made approach ensures our smart chatbots perfectly fit our clients' needs," says Antoine.

[Funding History]

Seed

After bootstrapping for the first nine months, FinChatBot has raised two rounds of seed funding totaling 8.6 million ZAR ($600,000), the most recent of which was a 7 million ZAR ($490,000) round late last year.

[Milestones]

- Publicly launching in June 2017 after a three-month market study in Cape Town.
- Relocating to Johannesburg the next month to establish the startup's first office space.
- Raising our first round of seed funding, allowing the business to get off the ground.
- Raising our second round in 2018 to cement our position at home and look further afield.

[Links] Web: **finchatbot.com** Twitter: **@finchatbot** LinkedIn: **company/finchatbot**

[Name] # Fixxr

[Elevator Pitch] *"We're an online platform that connects car owners to experienced mechanics in their area who come to homes and workplaces to carry out repairs."*

[The Story] The idea for mechanics marketplace Fixxr was conceived of when founder and CEO Curtis Young experienced the trials associated with fixing his own vehicle on short notice. After problems with both his car dealer and "backyard" mechanics, he decided to create a consistent, transparent process that would allow users to manage the maintenance of their car on their own terms while working closely with affiliated, professional and flexible mechanics. "Servicing your car if it's out of warranty is a painful, inconvenient process," says Curtis. "As a car owner, you're very often left feeling frustrated, inconvenienced and disempowered. That is the gap that Fixxr aims to address."

It has addressed it so successfully that in the ten months since its first customer, it facilitated around 250 services, generating over 300,000 ZAR ($21,000) worth of revenue for its mechanics and parts suppliers. Fixxr pre-negotiates labor rates so its customers don't have to and takes a 25 percent commission on any successfully completed work. Fixxr's offering is relevant everywhere, and it plans to be in Centurion and Pretoria before the end of 2019. "Our only current competition is traditional workshops, where car owners need to bring their cars in to get any work done and must pay for that inconvenience, or your backyard mechanics, who are more flexible but lack systems and processes," Curtis says.

[Funding History]

Bootstrap   Seed

Fixxr was bootstrapped until January 2019 when it won an IBM Bootcamp to take home seed funding of 500,000 ZAR ($35,500).

[Milestones]
- Servicing our first client in April 2018, marking the beginning of the Fixxr story.
- Reaching the one-hundred-completed-services mark in November 2018 – a major validation of our product.
- Winning the IBM bootcamp, which gave us access to seed funding and valuable exposure.
- Hiring our first employee in March 2019, demonstrating our growth as a company and increasing our capacity.
- Being selected to represent the South African delegation at the ITU Conference held in Durban in 2018.

[Links] Web: **fixxr.co.za** Facebook: **fixxrsa** Twitter: **@fixxrSA** LinkedIn: **company/fixxrsa**

[Name]

Homefarm

[Elevator Pitch]

"We are the creators of Homefarm, an indoor-gardening and food-growing platform. We empower and inspire you to grow the healthiest and most delicious plant-based foods and to enjoy the benefit of growing all year round."

[The Story]

Homefarm is a smart-home appliance and IoT platform that gives users the ability to grow their own food at home. Homefarm's CEO and founder Michael Currin created Homefarm in 2016 after completing a master's degree at the Royal College of Art's Innovation Design Engineering course in London. As a student, he became interested in the concept of empowering urban dwellers through the design of resilient, point-of-use solutions. "I have a passion for empowering people to break away from broken, overly centralized systems," he says. He believed that Homefarm would help people, especially those living in densely populated urban environments, to enjoy some independence from the unhealthy and inefficient modern food supply chain. "Homefarm aims to partner with influencers, brands and professionals in the health and wellness space to provide them with a platform for empowering their followers to enjoy the power of plants," says Michael.

The appliance, a smart micro-greenhouse that can connect to the internet via your wifi, is designed to grow nutritious microgreens and other produce, and it's paired with an app for tracking produce growth and learning recipes. Homefarm as a platform allows "foodies, gardeners, eco-warriors and health gurus" to fulfill their health and eco-conscious aspirations. Every crop type grown in a Homefarm has unique health benefits, and it uses paper-based packaging. Its consumable waste is biodegradable and compostable.

[Funding History]

Angel   External   Pre-Seed   Seed

Homefarm initially received pre-seed investment to complete an IndieGoGo campaign. Its campaign was one of the biggest in South Africa, finishing at $45,000. After that, it raised a seed round from angel investors, and will raise another seed round to commercialize in an international market. Homefarm receives revenue with sales of appliances, seeds and consumables.

[Milestones]

- Successfully completing our IndieGoGo campaign in July 2017.
- Completing the shipment of all units to crowdfunding donors.
- Finishing our design of the Homefarm appliance for manufacture and sale in July 2018.
- Launching our online store in October 2018.

[Links]

Web: **myhomefarm.io** Facebook: **homefarmnews** Instagram: **homefarm.news**

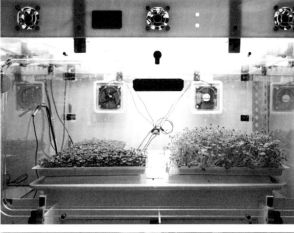

[Name]

InvestSure

[Elevator Pitch]

"We created an insurance product that insures listed shares bought on participating trading platforms against losses arising out of the deceptive or misleading acts of management of the company."

[The Story]

Back in 2016, Shane Curran had just finished training as an accountant and was looking to get involved in the investment space. He observed the fallout from the Volkswagen emissions scandal, which saw investors lose a lot of money, and noted that while there were plenty of products to help the management of investment firms caught up in these scandals, there were few solutions for ordinary investors. "We set out to change that," says Shane. InvestSure was conceptualized as a result of a Hannover Re innovation competition and initially rolled out exclusively on trading platform Easy Equities, where investors can insure their shares automatically as they buy them and also insure their existing portfolio.

The product, which covers losses in share price caused by allegations of management misleading or deceiving shareholders, is a world-first innovation, says Shane. "The beauty is that we automated the whole process; the customer doesn't have to do anything other than tick a box." InvestSure already has around three thousand policies purchased and has plans to expand, meaning it will soon be available on alternative trading platforms. "Uptake has been pretty good volume-wise," he says. "Now we're in the process of finding additional partners, both in South Africa and international markets." Australia and the UK are the immediate targets for expansion, though the main focus will remain on growing in South Africa.

[Funding History]

External   Seed

Originally funded by an insurance firm Compass Insure, InvestSure has just secured VC funding in order to expand. The funding totals around $1 million, raised from three different investors, providing about eighteen months runway for the business.

[Milestones]

- Winning a Bank of America Merrill Lynch competition with 1 million ZAR ($70,000) in prize money.
- Launching our initial product in an exclusive deal with trading platform Easy Equities.
- Reaching one thousand sales (and validating our product) barely three months after launching.
- Securing funding to allow expansion in South Africa and into new markets.

[Links]   Web: **investsure.info** Twitter: **@InvestsureZA** LinkedIn: **InvestSure**

[Name] # Kenai

[Elevator Pitch]

"We leverage facial recognition to give companies a single insightful picture of everyone in their building, improving safety, security and efficiency in an elegant way."

[The Story]

"We noticed the management of different people within corporate buildings was fractured, the sign-in process in particular, which was expensive for these businesses," says James Lightbody, cofounder of Kenai, which helps corporates better manage their business processes. "We wanted to facilitate the management of all these people in a better way." Its first product leverages facial recognition on an iPad application to recognize visitors when they arrive and automatically log their entry. Allowing visitors access via a facial scan means they only have to take part in a one-off process, creating a better experience while improving security within corporate buildings. The team has also built in the ability for visitors to pre-register before they arrive, without the need for the visitor to download an app.

Kenai launched its visitor facial-recognition product in beta with Accenture in March of 2018, and the product is now also used by a host of corporate entities, including RCS and Nedbank CIB. It comes with several value-adding features, including automatic visitor-badge printing and host notifications, and it's white labeled to enhance the corporate's brand throughout the visitor journey. "The visitor solution is really our ambassador product. We're aiming for one solution that manages all people within an office building," says James. Kenai wants to expand across South Africa and is also looking at overseas markets.

[Funding History]

Bootstrap

The founding team chose not to raise funding too early, so Kenai is bootstrapped for now but plans to take on external funding towards the second half of 2019 as its business moves into the next stage.

[Milestones]

- Completing our beta installation at Accenture.
- Hitting the 15,000 sign-ins landmark, thus validating that our product worked.
- Completing our full visitor solution in January 2019, which gave us the runway to expand.
- Finishing the beta version worker-management solution in September 2018.

[Links]   Web: **kenai.co.za** LinkedIn: **company/kenai**

[Name] # Raphta

[Elevator Pitch] *"We're the deep-technology company behind the flagship general-purpose deep-learning Shuri platform, which is able to process, analyze and make decisions out of sensory data from connected devices to solve complex problems."*

[The Story] Raphta, an AI startup, is named after the first metropolis in Africa (a city in Azania that is sometimes referred to as the "Atlantis of Africa"). The company came about after a friend of founder, Tshidiso Radinne, was a victim of identity theft. "A lookalike went into one of the telco's stores and took out a twenty-thousand-rand phone contract using his information," says Tshidiso. "After a few months, my friend started getting calls asking why he hadn't paid. He was shocked, and it became a fraud case." This situation was only resolved when the guilty party was caught attempting fraud again, but Tshidiso resolved to prevent such scenarios occurring in the future.

The solution he found was facial recognition technology, which resulted in the creation of Raphta in 2017. Tshidiso developed technology linking an individual's personal information with their facial profile when onboarding. "It was a simple and obvious solution," he says. "There are no two people that are exactly alike, not even twins." This morphed into a more general-focus AI platform named Shuri, which analyzes data to solve problems in property development and in the building of smart cities. The platform is made available to other companies to build their own solutions on, with clients including mobile operator MTN. Raphta is developing new platforms all the time and planning expansion into other verticals and geographies.

[Funding History]

Seed

Initially seed-funded by IBM, Raphta is in the process of raising a second round of funding, which it will use to convert the healthy pipeline of potential customers it has built.

[Milestones]
- Establishing a research and development collaboration agreement with the University of Witwatersrand.
- Being appointed as a Microsoft 4Afrika AI enablement partner, which was great validation for our business.
- Forming a commercial partnership to make the Shuri platform available on the Oracle Cloud platform.
- Seeing uptake of the Shuri platform by two of the leading telecoms companies in Africa.

[Links] Web: **raphta.com** LinkedIn: **company/raphta**

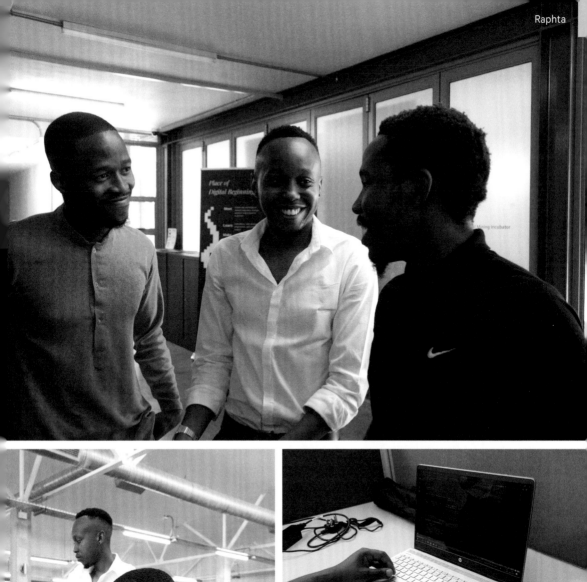

[Name]
Syafunda

[Elevator Pitch]

"We're a learning and data-management platform providing access to digital content through mobile technology."

[The Story]

Syafunda provides high schools with access to video, audio and ebook content through a wireless digital library and monitors student performance through digital tests to smooth educational processes. The edtech startup was launched in 2014 based on CEO Zakheni Ngubo's experiences at school in Umlazi. "We had very limited access to educational resources and information in a school that did not have a mathematics teacher during my final two years," he says. Zakheni set out to fill such gaps with the launch of Syafunda's "Black Box," which comes preloaded with digital content from various partners and allows students to download ebooks, video tutorials, past papers and worksheets. "What we've developed is an efficient and cost-effective content-distribution network without internet infrastructure," he says.

By integrating with the Department of Education and forming partnerships with stakeholders such as Old Mutual, PILO and the National Education Collaboration Trust (NECT), Syafunda has built a footprint of forty-seven schools in KwaZulu-Natal and Gauteng. Its goal is to grow further and make quality digital educational content more accessible to more students. The startup is looking to expand its reach with the launch of Syafunda Plus, which makes content available outside of schools, for example to community centers and libraries. "This will help us in expanding the experience and diversifying the reach," says Zakheni.

[Funding History]

Seed

Syafunda has so far raised 2.1 million ZAR ($150,000) in equity funding from a host of angel investors which has allowed it to develop digital content for math and science high school curricula. It is partly funded by the Shuttleworth Foundation and Virgin Unite.

[Milestones]

- Winning the global "Disrupt for Good" competition by Virgin Unite was a major landmark.
- Being accepted into the Pearson Affordable Learning Program gave us access to funding and support.
- Being rolled out in KZN schools was a vital step.
- Participating in Africa's first edtech accelerator Injini helped us further adapt our model.

[Links] Web: **syafunda.co.za** Facebook: **Syafunda** Twitter: **@syafunda** LinkedIn: **company/syafunda**

[Name]
Tuta-Me

[Elevator Pitch]
"We're an edtech company that aims to provide quality education across the country, regardless of wealth, through the use of technology."

[The Story]
Founded in 2015, Tuta-Me's initial product, rolled out in March 2016, was an "Uber for tutoring," connecting learners in need of academic assistance with highly qualified tutors. The startup excelled in a hackathon run by the City of Johannesburg and secured angel funding. It saw a positive initial uptake and has since grown to serve a wider need. It now offers online learning programs to Grade 8–12 learners in math, physical science and English, and it allows corporate entities to sponsor bursary students with tutor sessions. "Our core mission is to provide academic services to learners by enabling access to highly qualified tutors to improve understanding, knowledge and academic performance," says cofounder Dylan Hyslop.

The switch of focus from B2C to B2B, which focuses on fewer clients with bigger impact, has been a successful one, and Tuta-Me now has around 2,300 learners through companies, including the likes of Investec, Deloitte and Shell. Dylan says that the switch was beneficial in revenue terms, as businesses like these have larger budgets than individual consumers in South Africa. Now the plan is to keep building its technology and add more content and partners to spread availability. "Our vision is to become the most accessible, reliable and successful edtech company in South Africa," he says.

[Funding History]

Angel   Seed

Tuta-Me has raised two rounds of funding: one angel round in 2016 to help it develop its concept and the second one in 2018 from a larger education company.

[Milestones]
- Placing second in the Hack.Jozi accelerator in 2016.
- Raising our first round of funding, which validated our concept and gave us the runway to build out our platform.
- Pivoting in 2018 to a B2B business model, making Tuta-Me more sustainable in the long term.
- Securing high-caliber clients such as Deloitte, Honeywell, Shell and Investec.

[Links]   Web: **tuta-me.com** Facebook: **tutame123** Twitter: **@tuta_me** Instagram: **tuta_me_sa**

UNTIL
IT'S
DONE.

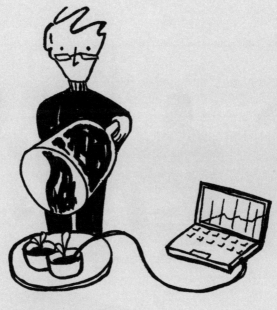

rams

- **Have a unique value proposition.**
  Show us that you have a unique and potentially industry-changing business offering or concept.

- **Have a strong team with all the necessary skills.**
  We're looking for high-quality entrepreneurial management with the requisite capabilities to execute on the business.

- **Be scalable.**
  We want startups to have local and international scalability, demonstrating the potential to scale to new geographies.

- **Focus on financial services.**
  We are a niche program in that we require startups to have a financial-services-focused offering, though this also includes innovations for regulatory services in financial services.

[Name]

AlphaCode Incubate

[Elevator Pitch]

"We are a mentor and grant-funding support program for standout concept or early-stage financial services businesses that are at least 51 percent Black-owned and have validated their business idea."

[Sector]

Fintech

[Description]

In 2015, South African financial services investment company Rand Merchant Investment (RMI) Holdings recognized that the core business of its underlying portfolio companies was being threatened by new and disruptive ventures and industry developments. It decided to find, fund and scale new and disruptive business models. The result was AlphaCode, a club for fintech startups established to support them and identify key investments that would change the landscape of the industry. It does this via a host of programs, namely through the data-science-training program Explore, the scale-up program Accelerate, and the early-stage program Incubate. "Our guide is to identify, partner and grow extraordinary financial services entrepreneurs," says Andile Maseko, head of ecosystem development at AlphaCode.

The Incubate program offers mentorship and grant funding to early-stage fintech companies, with the whole package worth 2 million ZAR ($140,000). Launched in partnership with Merrill Lynch South Africa and Royal Bafokeng Holdings, the twelve-month program also offers access to business-support services and networks as well as free office space in the heart of Sandton. It's open to entrepreneurs with innovative financial services business models in spaces such as payments, insurance, savings and investments, advisory, data analytics and blockchain.

The wider goal of Incubate, and of AlphaCode in general, is to contribute to building a thriving financial services entrepreneurial ecosystem in South Africa. It has positioned itself as a leader in both knowledge sharing and effective incubation, allowing it access to promising next-generation startups. "These can help optimize the operations of our portfolio businesses or be investee businesses that bolster our portfolio," says Andile. "Outside of our programs, we look to collaborate with startups that offer unique value to the Rand Merchant Investments portfolio of companies while also scouting for businesses that fit our investment mandate."

[Apply to]

alphacodeincubate.club

[Links]

Web: **alphacodeincubate.club** Facebook: **alphacodeclub** Twitter: **@alphacode_club**

- **Be an early-stage business focused on creative arts.**
  We're looking for participants who are actively
  involved in an early-stage, operational, arts-sector
  business.

- **Show high levels of motivation.**
  We interview all our candidates to ensure they have
  the required levels of motivation to see the program
  through.

- **Have an independent business mind.**
  You may be a creative individual, but we're also
  looking for evidence that you are independently
  business minded.

- **Be teachable.**
  You should approach all aspects of the program
  with an open mind and be willing to learn and take
  on board external advice and feedback.

[Name]
Creative Enterprises Hub

[Elevator Pitch]
"We're a business-development program for creative entrepreneurs to assist them in acquiring relevant professional and business skills and accessing the market and finance."

[Sector]
Creative arts

[Description]
In 2017, Mvuyo Ngqulana was part of the team running the South African leg of the Creative Business Cup, a global year-round initiative that empowers entrepreneurs in the creative industries. What he saw convinced him to cofound the Creative Enterprises Hub development program for creative entrepreneurs, as it was clear they needed more help than was available at the time. "It was apparent from the events' bootcamps that many creative entrepreneurs needed a lot of support for their businesses to be sustainable and profitable," says Mvuyo.

The program supports any full-time entrepreneur in the creative arts sector, such as graphic novelists, videographers, furniture designers, jewelry designers, mural artists, actors, musicians and graphic designers. It's based around short, flexibly structured events that it calls #Huddles, each of which caters to around twenty people. It helps participants deal with challenges that are specific to creative businesses, training them through workshops on how to make their companies more sustainable, find more business opportunities, and raise finance. "The program provides emerging and established creative businesses with an environment that supports their startup or growth phase and increases their likelihood of success," says Mvuyo. "The main goal is to produce successful businesses that leave the program financially viable and freestanding."

The premise is that creatives need more than just business-skills training. "They also need advice, mentorship and guidance, mental health and peer support, innovative networking and sourcing of business opportunities, and, of course, money," says Mvuyo. Creative Enterprises Hub provides a forum where arts entrepreneurs can meet, share challenges and opportunities, promote their offerings, explore collaboration, brainstorm ideas and learn relevant business skills. In order to achieve the right mix of participants, the program employs diagnostic screening to select those who are independently business minded, and it requires candidates to enter into a financial-commitment agreement.

[Apply to]
creativeenterpriseshub.co.za

[Links]
Web: **creativeenterpriseshub.co.za** Facebook: **CreativeBizHub** Twitter: **@CreativeBizHub**

- **Be founder-led.**
  Your business should have a strong founder or team of founders who have leadership potential and the vision to see your business scale exponentially.

- **Have ecosystem impact.**
  As a scaleup, your company should be a strong role model for other businesses in the ecosystem. You must be willing to give back to the program and commit to being a collaborative participant.

- **Have growth potential.**
  You should have a strong annual turnover that has the potential for growth. Endeavor's sweet spot for scaleups is a turnover preferably of at least $5 million and up to $10 million. Also, your IP or value proposition must be scalable globally.

- **Be at a key inflection point.**
  For Endeavor, timing is very important. Your scaleup should be at a key inflection point in your trajectory; meaning, your product or solution should be ready to enter an international market. This is especially essential for passing the international selection panel.

Endeavor South Africa

[Name]

[Elevator Pitch]

"We are the leading supporter of high-impact entrepreneurs around the world. With the world's best global network of entrepreneurs, mentors, funders and advisors, we work to catalyze long-term economic growth by selecting, mentoring and accelerating high-impact entrepreneurs worldwide."

[Sector]

Fintech, edtech, healthtech, enterprise software solutions, other tech verticals

[Description]

Endeavor is not a program in the traditional sense. Founded in 1997, it's a global nonprofit support network for entrepreneurs in the scaleup phase. Entrepreneurs that qualify with Endeavor receive bespoke mentorship, access to funding and talent and other types of support. Endeavor South Africa's chapter, which was founded in 2004 in parallel with government initiatives to drive the growth of SMEs, operates from offices in Johannesburg and Cape Town, guiding scaleups toward the right channels for scaling. "We are dedicated to helping scaleups with the biggest potential to impact their local ecosystems and grow their business," says Managing Director Alison Collier.

To become an Endeavor entrepreneur and join the network, scaleups must pass two selection panels. First, they present themselves to a local selection panel. Those that pass this stage receive limited access to local and international mentoring for six to nine months in order to prepare for the next phase: presenting to the international selection panel. Scaleups that pass through the international panel become part of the Endeavor network and are provided with special mentorship programs tailored to their specific needs. "We provide access to the right people in new markets," says Alison. "We're the bridge to the international community." This is especially beneficial for South African scaleups, as the ecosystem there is relatively small.

As well as tailormade mentoring, Endeavor offers connections to international business schools such as Harvard, Stanford and MIT. Scaleups can enroll in degree courses at discounted rates and can bring on MBA teams from these schools to work in their business pro bono for up to six months. Endeavor provides industry tours to introduce entrepreneurs to new markets and peers, and entrepreneurs also get access to investment via the Endeavor Catalyst Fund, a coinvesting "harvest fund" (in which they follow a lead VC in coinvesting) designed to support Endeavor entrepreneurs. Scaleups that do become Endeavor entrepreneurs are asked to give back in the form of a small financial contribution as well as providing mentorship to other entrepreneurs, thereby enhancing the network.

[Apply to]

endeavor.co.za

[Links]

Web: **endeavor.co.za** Facebook: **EndeavorSA** Twitter: **@EndeavorSA** Instagram: **endeavorsa**

- **Have a prototype.**
  The Innovation Hub prefers to start the incubation
  process at the prototype stage and beyond.
  You should already have a prototype to be eligible
  for The Innovation Hub's programs.

- **Understand your market.**
  You should put in a ton of research to make sure
  your innovation has the right market fit. Show keen
  insight into your market and be able to demonstrate
  what you're bringing to the fore.

- **Put together a solid team.**
  Your ideas and innovations will only be as good
  as the team that develops them. You should put
  together a proactive and passionate team that
  shares your vision.

- **Be resilient yet flexible.**
  Most importantly, you should have the discipline,
  patience and resilience to see this process through.
  On the flip side, you should have the humility to work
  well with a mentor and be willing to let go of your idea
  if need be.

[Name]
The Innovation Hub

[Elevator Pitch]
"We are a science and technology park and an innovation agency working to foster the economic development and competitiveness of the Gauteng Province."

[Sector]
Green economy (water, energy and waste management), smart industries (ICT and advanced manufacturing), bio-economy (health and agro-processing)

[Description]
Established by the Gauteng Provincial Government to foster innovation and entrepreneurship in the region, The Innovation Hub offers a myriad of incubator programs. As a science and technology park built for the entire region, it offers innovation programs and development on site as well as in townships throughout Gauteng Province. The main goal of The Innovation Hub is to make innovation accessible. "We're trying to take away all the hurdles," says Matona Sakupwanya, the hub's general manager of Marketing and Communications. "Innovation waits for no one."

The Innovation Hub has four distinct incubators, three in-house (MAXUM, BioPark, CIC SA) and one external (eKasiLab), each split into two programs, depending on the stage of prospective entrepreneurs and startups. Pre-revenue or pre-commercialization companies can join the Factory Program, a twelve-month program that focuses on assisting companies with product development, market access and market testing for technology. Once companies have commercialized and made their first sales, they qualify for the Core Program, a three-year post-revenue program aimed at assisting commercialized companies to scale up and grow. The focus is on local and international market growth, investment attraction and business linkages. Once the company has demonstrated profitability and sustainability based on scaled-up operational capacity and sales, the startup is graduated out of the Core Program. Both program stages offer incubated startups access to advisory and skills development, markets, infrastructure and funding and networking opportunities.

There is also a rich network of partners to help build the ecosystem. "Through our government and corporate network, we assist with linkages to funding access," says Matona. "We foster a conducive environment by creating various networking opportunities and platforms so startups and partners can engage with one another." Alongside their three in-house incubators, The Innovation Hub brings support to township-based entrepreneurs through eKasiLabs, which provides business-development support to startups in the Hub's priority sectors in various townships in Gauteng through collaboration with local government and academic institutions.

[Apply to]
info@theinnovationhub.com

[Links]
Web: **theinnovationhub.com** Facebook: **InnovHubZA** Twitter: **@InnovHub**

- Have an innovative idea or early-stage business in the media space.
  We are looking for proposals capable of disrupting the existing media landscape or reaching communities not adequately served by existing media.

- Solve a problem.
  We want a big idea that solves a real journalism or media problem in the marketplace.

- Have a solid team.
  We encourage people to apply as a team of at least two people able to commit all or a substantial majority of their time to their project.

- Be passionate about journalism and media.
  Your idea or venture could be about making data or knowledge more useful and accessible, or enabling debate and comment.

- Have a working prototype or at least show you're at the right stage.
  We're looking for innovators with a great idea and the commitment to create and sustain a new journalism or media venture.

[Name]

JamLab

[Elevator Pitch]

"We are Africa's first journalism and media accelerator, offering media entrepreneurs the facilities, tools and networks necessary to scale their ventures."

[Sector]

Media

[Description]

An Africa-first, the JamLab (The Journalism and Media Lab) accelerator is a six-month hothouse program for journalists and media innovators, helping them realize their ambitions by providing the relevant tools, facilities, contacts and support. It targets journalism and media startups as well as members of the media who want to launch a new product or service. Tshepo Tshabalala, web editor at JamLab, stresses its uniqueness. "We tap into the media space, which is often overlooked and not well represented in the entrepreneurial ecosystem," he says. "The program also puts a lot of emphasis on tech application and innovation, which is an under-developed sphere in the African media context."

Selected teams receive a free workspace as well as mentorship and coaching from experienced media, startup and tech experts. They first take part in a two-week bootcamp to align expectations for the program, build relationships between the teams, introduce key working methods and assess each team's support and mentorship needs. The rest of the program assists entrepreneurs in building out their products and connecting them with the relevant people to help their media businesses grow. "We offer access to software-development experts and opportunities to meet and pitch to potential investors and funders," says Tshepo.

Selected media startups also have the opportunity to attend a Wits University–accredited, three-month media entrepreneurship course called "Creating the Media." JamLab is funded by an ever-changing selection of donors, and although it can provide only limited funding support for tech development, it does offer more hands-on development assistance. In addition, at the end of the program, teams have the opportunity to pitch to potential investors at a demo day. Tshepo says JamLab has accelerated twelve startups since its inception in 2017, with standout companies being Volume News and Media Factory. "Overall, the JamLab accelerator program aims to move the teams' proposed innovations to a point where they are all investable. This requires developing and testing at least a basic version of their product or service and researching and testing the market for their service."

[Apply to]

jamlab.africa

[Links]

Web: **jamlab.africa** Facebook: **jamlabafrica** Twitter: **@jamlabafrica**

- **Have a unique value proposition.**
  Show us that you have a clearly identified problem
  and have come up with a unique way of solving it.

- **Show us your traction.**
  Your business needs to have moved beyond the idea
  stage and have a proof of concept and validation.

- **Have a long-term vision.**
  We are looking for creative entrepreneurs who think
  big and have a vision of where they want to see their
  business down the line.

- **Contribute to our community.**
  You'll need to demonstrate what you'll bring to the
  J&B Hive community and how you'll fit in with our
  mantras: "Give and get given," "Get it out there,"
  "Never stop learning," "Seek opportunities,"
  "Be profit-oriented," and "Get social."

[Name]

J&B Hive Accelerator

[Elevator Pitch] *"We are a catalyst for creative entrepreneurs, allowing those on a mission to disrupt the market to connect, collaborate and celebrate, and catering to their business-support needs with a range of infrastructure, workshops, masterclasses and access to business specialists."*

[Sector] **Creative**

[Description] Clare Beaumont-Adam wanted to develop entrepreneurs and provide them with the right support to make their business vision a reality, and she wanted to do this working with brands with a passion for collaborating with millennials. J&B Hive launched with the backing of J&B Scotch Whisky in 2015. Its vision – to develop and inspire creative entrepreneurs – aligned well with the ethos of the whisky brand. "The brand is entrepreneurial, and it fed into the work that we wanted to do," says director Sibongile Musundwa. "J&B is looking to collaborate and create content around the change this generation is driving – it's seen as the whisky brand that's at the heart of millennial culture."

The J&B Hive takes a wide definition of "creative," focusing on businesses innovating in culture and socializing in spaces such as digital innovation, design, fashion, film, music, publishing, food and marketing. One level of membership is through its J&B Hive Accelerator, a program that offers office space, equity-free funding, workshops, one-on-one engagements and mentorship. Though there's no cost to enter the program, there is a stringent application process. Creative businesses need to have moved beyond the idea stage and be able to regularly attend the J&B Hive for sessions and events.

The program, says Sibongile, balances a belief in the entrepreneur with a belief in the business. Its content is honed particularly towards creatives, and it taps into a community of like-minded people at J&B Hive. This community is at the heart of everything the J&B Hive is trying to build in its Braamfontein space. "We're growing a community, so it's not about just one business but about getting through things together. It's all about the network effect. We're looking for entrepreneurs with vision, that have a long-term goal for their business."

[Apply to] thejbhivejohannesburg.com

[Links] Web: **thejbhivejohannesburg.com** Facebook: **hivejoburg** Twitter: **@hivejoburg** Instagram: **hivejoburg**

- **Be fully focused.**
  We're looking for entrepreneurs that are active within their businesses on a full-time basis.

- **Be relentless and persevere.**
  Participants in our programs should have the relentless ability to stand up again and again.

- **Be flexible.**
  Unexpected challenges appear constantly and entrepreneurs need to be flexible in their thinking so they can quickly recover from setbacks.

- **Be willing to learn.**
  You should see problems as learning opportunities and using the lessons gained to develop and refine ideas.

- **Show curiosity.**
  A wide-ranging curiosity about how the world works strengthens the ability to think laterally.

- **Have a high internal locus of control.**
  Show faith in your own ability to determine your success.

[Name]

Raizcorp

[Elevator Pitch]

"We are an incubator that provides full-service enterprise and supplier development programs that guide entrepreneurs to profitability."

[Sector]

Multisector

[Description]

Founded in 2000, Raizcorp describes itself as a "prosperator," an organization that supports entrepreneurs to prosperity by using sophisticated methodologies evolved over twenty years. It says it has created its own unique model of business incubation, through which it supports entrepreneurs through all stages of development via a host of different programs, providing training and guidance that can be translated into practical business success. Since its launch, Raizcorp has incubated over 13,000 businesses. "We are currently supporting five hundred businesses at our twelve incubators in South Africa, Angola, Tanzania and Zimbabwe," says CEO Allon Raiz.

The most important element in Raizcorp's approach to supporting startups is the selection of these companies. Every day, Raizcorp receives between fifty and one hundred applications to join one of its programs, with these applicants put through a rigorous eight-step selection process in which one in twenty is successful. Once the entrepreneur has been chosen, they are allocated to an appropriate program that suits their stage, size and even their sector. The fully sponsored, high-touch incubation programs provide entrepreneurial learning and business guidance with five dedicated mentors, who focus on sales, marketing, finance, personal development and strategy. "In addition, entrepreneurs receive access to markets, access to specialists, access to infrastructure, back-office support and access to finance," says Allon.

Raizcorp provides corporate sponsors with access to quality suppliers for enterprise and supplier development, and it funds its programs in two ways. The first is through its Partner Elite division, where it takes equity in specific types of businesses and funds the business through dividends and a small fee. It also allows corporates to pay for bursaries for entrepreneurs to go through its programs. Over the years, Allon says it has developed a number of extremely successful entrepreneurial businesses. "One of our most recent and successful cohorts comprises five companies who participated in the De Beers-Raizcorp diamond-beneficiation project. This pilot project was a resounding success."

[Apply to]

raizcorp.com

[Links]

- **Prove your viability.**
  We're looking for concepts where there is evidence of demand and indications that the business model is sound.

- **Have an entrepreneurial spirit.**
  You should display entrepreneurial characteristics and demonstrate an ability to get things done.

- **Show local potential.**
  Your product or solution must come with evidence of economic potential for the local area.

- **Have a positive cost–benefit ratio.**
  Riversands Incubation Hub looks for the highest returns on its investment of support and subsidized square meters, which we measure in terms of social good and economic value unlocked.

[Name]
Riversands Incubation Hub

[Elevator Pitch]
"We're a large-scale business incubator that helps entrepreneurs grow through access to office space and quality support services."

[Sector]
Sector agnostic

[Description]
Launched in 2015, the nonprofit Riversands Incubation Hub aims to act as a bridge between small businesses and corporates in South Africa. It offers customized support to business owners according to the size and maturity of their business and their needs at any given point. Support is offered in broad categories of premises, market access and back office as well as training and business coaching. "We're an ambitious social enterprise with the scale to make a real difference," says CEO Jenny Retief. "With over one hundred sixty workshops, factories and offices, we help early-stage businesses grow through professional premises, market-access assistance, and back-office administration services."

Apart from the support pillar of premises, the most frequently requested services are assistance with bookkeeping and financial management and market access support, which ranges from the basics, such as getting a professional company profile, logo and product photographs in place, to a full marketing strategy, public-relations assistance and introductions to supply-chain opportunities with corporate partners. "Our approval process and SME Support System allow us to monitor impact and ensure we invest our support wisely," says Jenny.

Though still early stage, all the SMEs on the Riversands campus have reached the point where they can afford to pay the subsidized rental. A flexible, entrepreneur-friendly lease allows them to move out, or downscale or upscale premises at short notice. Each business taking part in the program has a service coordinator assigned to them when they first occupy premises, which makes it fast and easy for entrepreneurs to request the specific support their business needs. "In some instances, SMEs request a business mentor," says Jenny, "and Riversands Incubation Hub is privileged to have a number of experienced coaches and mentors, including volunteer mentors who draw on their business networks and experience to help business owners navigate the market and grow their businesses."

[Apply to]
riversandsihub.co.za

[Links]
Web: **riversandsihub.co.za** Facebook: **riversandshub** Twitter: **@RiversandsHub**

- **Have a viable model.**
  You must have a business idea or an early-stage business that is viable.

- **Know your market.**
  We are looking for entrepreneurs that have done market research and tested their product or service.

- **Meet our criteria.**
  We work with disadvantaged groups so our startups are usually women or youth-led.

- **Appeal to our corporate sponsors.**
  Usually, our sector focuses are driven by the corporate sponsor but can range from energy through to social creative businesses.

Seed Academy

[Name]

[Elevator Pitch] *"We help businesses to build, grow and scale by building the skills and capacity of entrepreneurs, funding and supporting them to grow their businesses, and working with corporate South Africa to take them to scale."*

[Sector] **Multi-sector**

[Description] Founded in 2013, Seed Engine has grown into a major player within the South African entrepreneurial landscape over the past few years. The organization takes a holistic and integrated approach to transformation and job creation, supporting entrepreneurs with business-development support, access to markets and access to funding. It does this by partnering with corporate clients to develop specific programs, as well as by always having the entrepreneurs' needs front and center. "We relentlessly fight for our entrepreneurs to get access to markets and funding opportunities whilst keeping our clients' business and transformation objectives and return on investment at heart," says CEO Donna Rachelson.

Seed Engine is made up of two main parts: Seed Academy and the WDB Growth Fund. The former provides high-impact business development support and access to markets to entrepreneurs at all stages, helping them to build successful, sustainable businesses. It runs a three-month, fully funded business accelerator for women, as well as Enterprise and Supplier Development programs that focus on ensuring businesses are ready to compete in corporate supply chains. The "Seed Way" is a systematic methodology "that moves entrepreneurs from build to grow and ultimately to scale," says Donna. Through its networks in the ecosystem and strong strategic and public-private partnerships, Seed Academy develops interventions that support entrepreneurs from a business and personal leadership development perspective while providing them with unprecedented access to market. "We also drive an acceleration mindset with a strong delivery focus, innovation mindset and robust attention to impact measurement."

The Seed Academy programs create a pipeline of funding-ready businesses for the WDB Growth Fund and corporate supply chains. The fund is a Section 12J Impact Investment Fund, focused on increasing the participation of youth and women entrepreneurs in South Africa's economy. The fund addresses the needs of growth-stage businesses while providing investors with enterprise- and supplier-development points recognition, tax benefits and a return on investment.

[Apply to] seedengine.co.za/entrepreneur-application-form

[Links] Web: **seedengine.co.za** Facebook: **seedenginesa** Twitter: **@seed_engine**

- **Identify a serious problem.**
  Your business should be tackling a major issue
  for your customers through the use of technology.

- **Show you can get stuff done.**
  We're looking for teams with a proven track
  record of execution.

- **Have an appetite for receiving feedback.**
  Entrepreneurs should be coachable and willing
  to learn from mentors and program partners.

- **Be in it for the long haul.**
  We want founders who are prepared for the long
  and potentially uncomfortable journey that is building
  a technology business in Africa.

Sw7

[Name]

[Elevator Pitch] *"We are Africa's first 'always open' acceleration platform. We offer technology businesses – from startup to scaleup – access to the resources they need, when they need them, to help them grow and scale."*

[Sector] **B2B technology, sector agnostic**

[Description] Sw7 is one of the best established accelerators in South Africa with over two hundred tech businesses accelerated through programs in Johannesburg and Cape Town and partnerships with corporates such as Microsoft and Standard Bank. The company also works with businesses at its Sandton coworking space and, in a recent change of approach, it launched an always-open model to offer on-demand support to as many entrepreneurs as possible across different geographies. "Anyone can join Sw7 at any time and get access to the help their business needs. This differs from most other programs that tend to be life-stage, agenda, time and location specific," says Odette Jones, who cofounded Sw7 alongside her husband Keith.

Sw7 works with technology businesses from a variety of sectors through the seven life stages (ideation, validation, productization, commercialization, growth, expansion and exit), helping younger companies with product-market fit, go-to-market strategies, business model generation, sales cycle management, and becoming investor-ready. For more established businesses, it does business valuations, fundraising, strategic board advisory and offshore structuring, and can also assist with expansion into the rest of Africa, the UK and the US. "We provide objective views of where the business is and where they need to move to, and we offer curated connections to partners and mentors," says Odette.

Sw7 technology partners include the likes of Microsoft, Amazon and Google, but the company also works with a host of other corporate entities in a variety of areas. Many of its services are offered to startups for free, but higher-touch elements are offered as a premium service. Its strength is in its outcomes-based performance-management approach and flexibility, with a focus on making Sw7 as accessible as possible to all kinds of technology businesses. Sw7 wants to assist not just the 1 percent that manage to get funded but the other 99 percent as well. "We're there for founders who are trying to build successful technology businesses in very challenging markets."

[Apply to] info@sw7.co

[Links] Web: **Sw7.co** Twitter: **@Sw7co** LinkedIn: **groups/8202897**

ces

[Name]
22 ON SLOANE

[Address]
22 Sloane Street, Bryanston, Johannesburg 2191

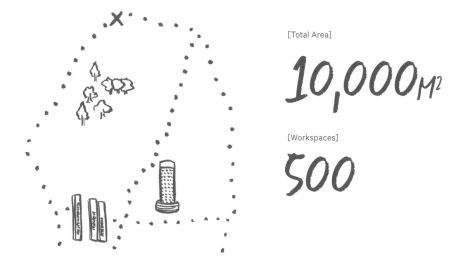

[Total Area]

10,000M²

[Workspaces]

500

[The Story]
22 ON SLOANE is the largest startup campus in Africa. It was launched in 2017 by the Global Entrepreneurship Network (GEN) Africa, which operates in forty-two nations on the continent and aims to help African entrepreneurs start and grow their business. The 22 ON SLOANE campus hosts a twelve-month residency program for selected startups in sectors such as agriculture, energy, IoT, finance, healthcare and manufacturing, all with an underlying focus on technology. It offers its residents a full, turnkey solution from ideation to commercialization and also rents out space to non-resident tenants and day visitors.

The campus is situated in the upscale, residential suburb of Bryanston with easy access to transport modes, retail centers and local business districts. The building itself was formerly occupied by a pharmaceutical company, and a large-scale renovation was needed to give 22 ON SLOANE its modern, vibrant startup feel. Resident startups have access to a dizzying range of amenities, including three tech labs, a 3D-printing option, four kitchen facilities, a selection of lounge rooms and boardrooms for meetings, a gym, a prayer room and even a much-needed siesta room. The heart of the building is the large, open atrium, which serves as a chillout and workspace by day and the main area for business and social events by night.

[Links]   Web: 22onsloane.co Facebook: GEN22ONSLOANE Twitter: @GEN22OnSloane

Face of the Space:
Gamuchirai Mutezo, the chief operations officer at GEN Africa – 22 ON SLOANE, is a strategist by nature. With a background in urban planning, renewable energy and waste, she has long been surrounded by budding entrepreneurs, and she was herself infected by the "entrepreneurial bug" from an early stage. Her main task is to ensure that everything runs smoothly at the campus; thus, she calls herself "the oil that makes the gears turn."

AlphaCode

[Name]

[Address] 2 Merchant Place, Cnr Fredman Drive and Rivonia Road, Sandton, Johannesburg 2196

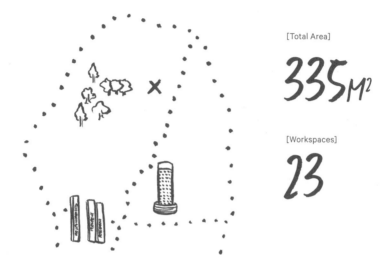

[Total Area]

335M²

[Workspaces]

23

[The Story] In September 2015, South African financial services investment company Rand Merchant Investment (RMI) Holdings launched AlphaCode, a club aimed at finding, funding and scaling innovative fintech startups. It all started with its members-only events and coworking space in Sandton, from which it now runs a host of programs and initiatives for fintech entrepreneurs. "We run a host of thought-leadership events and encourage startups within the space to work together in coming up with innovative financial solutions," says Andile Maseko, head of ecosystem development at AlphaCode. The modern, open, aesthetically appealing space has lots of clear glass and is designed for collaboration.

AlphaCode offers flex desk space for members in addition to dedicated offices for businesses taking part in its programs, while members also have access to boardrooms, wifi, printing and other general office amenities. Its location, just a short walk from Johannesburg's financial district, makes it easy to connect with corporates and other entrepreneurs in the financial services sector. While AlphaCode's dedicated programs help startups grow, the seeds of this growth and collaboration are sown in the space. "We're here to identify extraordinary entrepreneurs and partner with them to foster the development of startups and collaboration at the different business life stages," says Andile.

[Links] Web: **alphacode.club** Facebook: **alphacodeclub** Twitter: **@alphacode_club**

Face of the Space:
Andile Maseko, head of ecosystem
development at AlphaCode, is an
entrepreneur and helped to cofound
a small fintech business in 2017. Prior
to this, he was involved in consultancy
work for Cricket South Africa and
Paper Plane Ventures. He qualified as
a chartered accountant after serving
articles at Deloitte in Johannesburg.

[Name] # Impact Hub Joburg

[Address] 158 Jan Smuts Building, 9 Walters Street, Rosebank, Johannesburg 2196

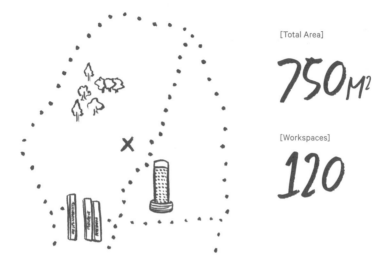

[Total Area]

750M²

[Workspaces]

120

[The Story] Impact Hub is a global network of hubs focused on fostering entrepreneurship, idea incubation and business development, as well as offering coworking spaces. All of its hubs are geared towards the impact innovation ecosystem and the Sustainable Development Goals (SDGs). There are more than one hundred Impact Hubs in over fifty countries worldwide, but in 2010, when Impact Hub Joburg opened its doors in Braamfontein, it was the first of its kind in Africa. The space has since moved to Rosebank, a more central location within walking distance of the Gautrain. It offers flexible workspaces, private offices, a double-volume event space, meeting rooms and a makerspace. "We are very focused on sharing and developing skills in our community. It's all about collaboration and cocreation, learning and breaking down silos," says CEO Thandi Dyani.

The Rosebank space is modern with high ceilings, natural wood, and a lot of glass. It offers impressive views of downtown Johannesburg and is home to a variety of organizations. Most are impact-focused businesses operating in a variety of spaces, but there is also a host of NGOs and non-impact businesses. "We firmly believe that changing businesses and society to create real positive impact requires inclusive and collective action. We collaborate with Hubbers and partners that we find aligned with our values and the SDGs," says Thandi.

[Links] Web: johannesburg.impacthub.net Facebook: impacthubjoburg Twitter: @impacthubjoburg

Face of the Space:
Before joining Impact Hub Joburg,
Thandi Dyani worked in the impact-startup,
social-entrepreneurship and global-
development fields for more than ten
years with a special focus on African affairs
and context. She has launched and led
an NGO and cofounded social-innovation
conferences and an impact accelerator
program. Currently, she leads the impact
venture-philanthropic investment efforts
of One Life Foundation.

[Name]

J&B Hive Creative Hub

[Address]   100 Juta Street, Braamfontein, Johannesburg 2000

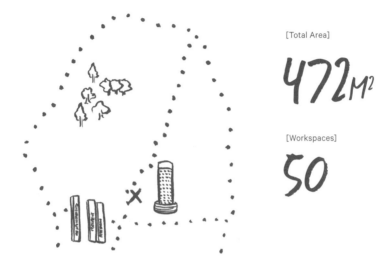

[Total Area]

472m²

[Workspaces]

50

[The Story]   Launched in 2015 on the fringes of trendy Braamfontein and funded by J&B Scotch Whisky, the J&B Hive is a community of creative entrepreneurs. The space, which also hosts an accelerator program for creative businesses, offers members coworking facilities, access to audiovisual equipment and entry to a variety of events. Members are creative entrepreneurs who come from fields ranging from music and fashion to the bar and cafe industries. Membership is free, but applicants are selected based on what value they can bring to the community and how the J&B Hive feels it can help tangibly grow that individual's business. "We believe in building this network, and giving creative entrepreneurs the opportunity to be around like-minded people," says director Sibongile Musundwa.

The space itself was originally home to a bank before becoming an art gallery, and its modern design is reminiscent of the latter. The open-plan, white-walled space has a mezzanine level for members, who also have access to a boardroom (which doubles as a production studio), an in-house cafe and evening bar. The space, which is within walking distance of Braamfontein's many cafes, bars, restaurants, shops and galleries, houses pop-up retail stores run by community members and doubles as an event venue by night, with a variety of events taking place every week from Wednesday to Saturday.

[Links]   Web: thejbhivejohannesburg.com Facebook: hivejoburg Twitter: @hivejoburg Instagram: hivejoburg

Face of the Space:

J&B Hive director Sibongile Musundwa
is a creative industries advocate and
project manager with networks spanning
over South Africa and the UK. Whether
it's through her work at Owning The Light,
J&B Hive or elsewhere, she creates
environments for those in arts, culture and
entrepreneurship to fulfill their potential
and – in some cases – make their dreams
come true.

JoziHub

[Name]

[Address]   44 Stanley Ave, Milpark, Johannesburg 2094

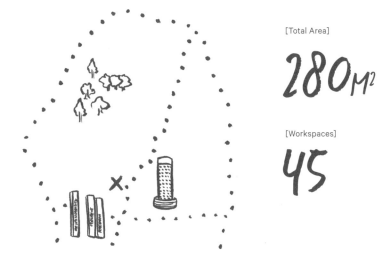

[Total Area]

280м²

[Workspaces]

45

[The Story]   An early mover in the Johannesburg coworking space, JoziHub launched in 2013 to help build a community and provide a fertile environment for tech startups in the city. It now runs more than 350 workshops and events for its community each year and provides a collaborative workspace for young tech entrepreneurs. The space, located in one of Johannesburg's design precincts, is surrounded by a selection of cafes, restaurants and bespoke design stores and businesses. Available for only 1,200 ZAR ($84) per person per month, it is priced for startups. "It provides startups with the opportunity to work alongside other entrepreneurs, which often results in collaboration and sharing of ideas and services," says founder Samantha Manclark.

In addition to attending workshops and events, JoziHub tenants can also access programs (including business-mentorship programs) through its various partnerships, and tools, workshops and a network of hubs and incubators across the globe via its link with Google for Startups. The twenty-four-hour space has a meeting room and two informal meeting areas, a large space for events or workshops that can fit up to one hundred people, and a coffee and snack bar. "Jozihub is a relaxed, modern, vibrant, work- and learning-focused environment," says Samantha. "There's a constant flow of people in and out of the JoziHub events space and coffee bar area."

[Links]   Web: jozihub.org Facebook: jozihub Twitter: @JoziHub Instagram: jozihub

Face of the Space:
Samantha Manclark is an entrepreneur in her own right, having founded and managed two successful PR and events companies after starting out in the advertising world at Hunt Lascaris TBWA. Her current business is A Better World Network, which provides strategic communications, PR and marketing services. She also heads up the team at JoziHub.

Perch Flexible Offices

[Name]

[Address] 37 Bath Ave, Rosebank, Johannesburg 2196

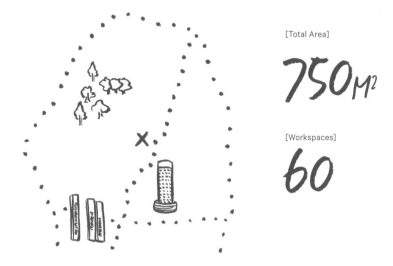

[Total Area]

750M²

[Workspaces]

60

[The Story] Perch Flexible Offices in Rosebank opened its doors in 2017 in order to meet the increasing demand for startup office space. Since then, it has grown steadily and now has twenty-two private offices, twenty dedicated desks and forty flexible coworking workstations alongside team booths, informal meeting areas and five meeting rooms. It offers reliable wifi, printing facilities, free coffee and access to a variety of events, and is used by a mix of entrepreneurs, small businesses and freelancers from a range of industries. "Perch gives businesses the opportunity to scale and evolve in an environment that fosters growth, and on flexible terms," says Mia Da Camara, the community and marketing manager at Perch.

The interior design of the space is homey and inviting, embracing a variety of complementary colors. The combination of warm vibrant tones blends with natural materials such as oak, and the environment is aimed at encouraging creative thinking and working. In addition to offering affordable, flexible workspace to entrepreneurs with limited budgets and uncertain futures, it's also a place to enjoy hanging out and networking. "It is space to engage with people who share similar ideas," says Mia, "and in this way, it creates an organic community where ideas and skills can be shared."

[Links] Web: perchoffices.co.za Facebook: PerchOffices Twitter: @PerchOffices Instagram: perch.offices

Face of the Space:

Mia Da Camara has spent most of her career working in marketing and communications, specializing in graphic design, UX design and web development. She lived in Singapore and Hong Kong and worked out of many different coworking spaces until leaving in 2015. On her return to Johannesburg, she founded a coworking space called Community Centre. Soon after it closed, she became the community and marketing manager at Perch Offices and found a happy balance in coworking again.

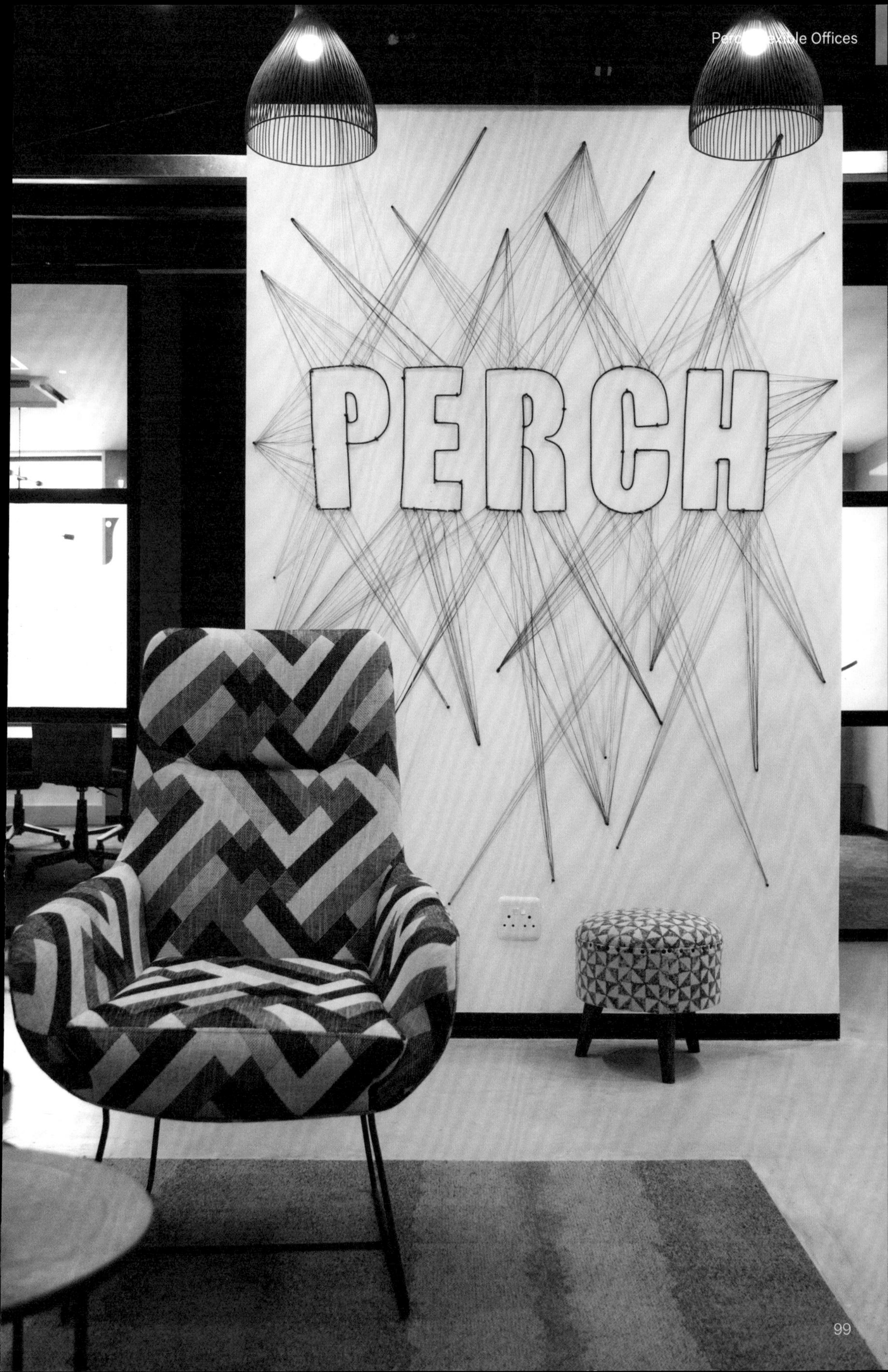
PERCH

Tshimologong Precinct

[Name]

[Address]   41 Juta Street, Braamfontein, Johannesburg 2001

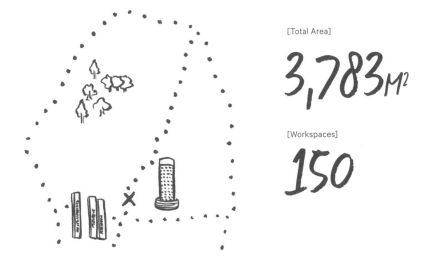

[Total Area]

3,783M²

[Workspaces]

150

[The Story]   Tshimologong Precinct is a central coworking space and tech hub founded in 2016 by professor Barry Dwolatzky, the director of the Johannesburg Centre of Software Engineering at Wits University. Located in the Braamfontein district right next to campus, Tshimologong ("new beginnings" in Setswana) offers entrepreneurs, students and makers a space to develop their innovations, start viable businesses and leverage the high-level research and resources of the university. Tshimologong is an enabler of tech and digital innovation, bringing together innovators, corporates and government through incubation programs, events and residencies.

The precinct is housed in four refurbished buildings, one of which was once a nightclub that still retains its vibrant and colorful decor despite having been repurposed. All furniture is modular, so the different spaces can dynamically fit membership needs. The coworking space itself, called the Accelerator, has hot desk access, meeting rooms, boardrooms, a kitchenette and a coffee shop. Tshimologong also offers a growing roster of enterprise-development programs and has a fully functional makerspace with VR and AR capabilities, 3D printers and laser cutters, so entrepreneurs can bring their ideas into the physical world. "It's quite dynamic and social," says member-experience coordinator Natalie Makgamathe. "The energy from the city and university makes people want to come and see what's happening next."

[Links]   Web: **tshimologong.joburg** Facebook: **TshimologongPrecinct** Twitter: **@TshimologongIT**

Face of the Space:

Prior to becoming the member-experience coordinator at Tshimologong, Natalie Makgamathe was a stage performer and puppeteer for nearly a decade. Not once did she imagine she would end up in tech. To immerse herself in the industry, she attended master classes at Tshimologong during Global Entrepreneurship Week 2017. Along with looking after the entrepreneurs' needs and fostering helpful synergies within the space, Natalie also loves refurbishing furniture.

[Name] # Workshop17 West Street

[Address] 138 West Street, Sandton, Johannesburg 2031

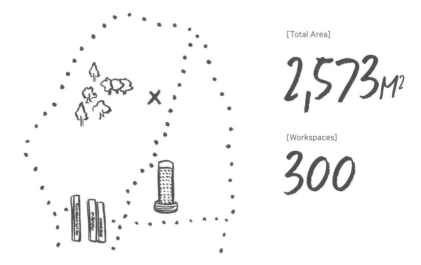

[Total Area]

2,573M²

[Workspaces]

300

[The Story] Part of a network of coworking spaces that began life in Maboneng in 2012 and now extends to Cape Town, Workshop17 West Street opened in Sandton in 2017. The three-floor location, which has space for members and nonmembers, offers private and flexible desk space, meeting rooms, boardrooms, a cafe and a 130-seat auditorium. It also features two communal kitchen areas, a silent hot-desking room, dedicated Skype rooms, mobile writable whiteboards and uncapped internet. Workshop17 is modern and spacious, offering tenants the freedom to move around and build connections. "There's a vibrant buzz to the space with people moving about and focusing on what is most important to their business," says Charl Ochler, the space's community manager. "Our vision is to become like a coral reef of innovation."

The space has a wide variety of tenants ranging from small startups to bigger organizations and focusing on sectors ranging from agritech to blockchain. Members include filmmakers, digital and social media specialists, brand and marketing specialists, lawyers, and digital innovation teams. All members become part of a wide community, giving them access to localized service providers and potential customers. "This opens up perspectives, insights and connections for them to build on their success," says Charl. "And because we provide flexibility, their business can grow and also shrink if need be without them being stuck in long-term contracts and limiting spaces."

[Links] Web: workshop17.co.za/sandton Facebook: workshop17 Twitter: @workshop17za

Face of the Space:
Charl Ochler, community manager
at Workshop17, previously worked
as a radio presenter and has starred
in various stage and film productions.
He also has a background in sales and
merchandising. After roles at PMI and
Varsity College Sandton, he joined
Workshop17 and is now responsible
for the well-being of all tenants in the
Sandton space.

erts

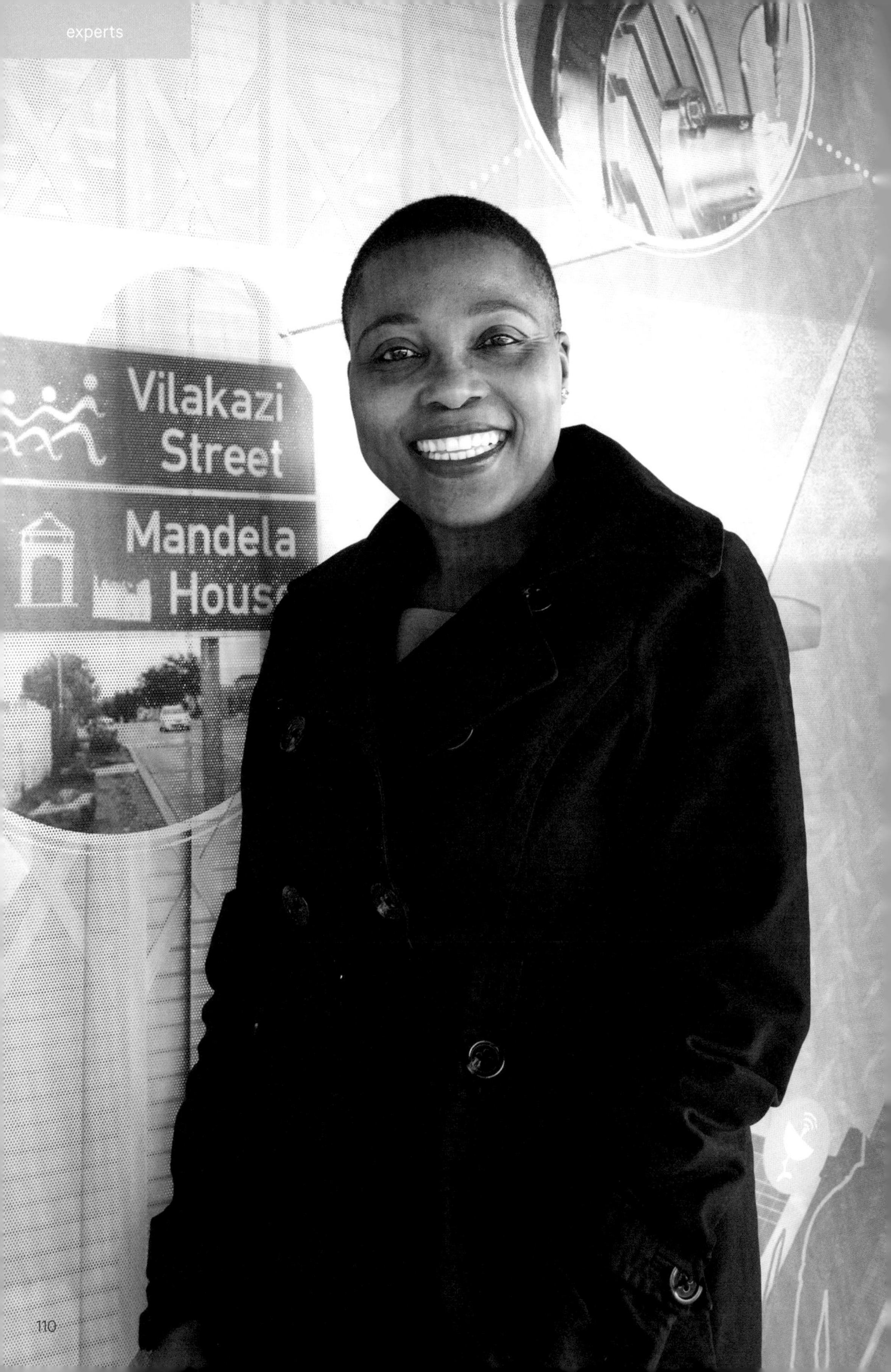
Vilakazi
Street
Mandela

Nothile Mpisi
/ eKasiLabs

General Manager

[Sector] **Smart industry (ICT and advanced manufacturing), bio-economy, green economy, creative economy, multimedia**

Innovation thrives in existing business infrastructures and ecosystems, and it's common to take this for granted. In hubs like Silicon Valley, Paris, Singapore and many others, there's an abundance of accelerators, incubators, networking events and funding sources, and the distance between talent and opportunity is not so insurmountable. In South Africa, however, there are regions (such as provincial townships) with little access to this sort of formalized development.

The Innovation Hub, an innovation agency and science park created to foster economic development and entrepreneurship in the Gauteng province, offers specialized support and access to entrepreneurs based in Gauteng's townships. One of its programs, the eKasiLabs incubator, brings innovation culture and the related benefits directly to townships and, in turn, often transports entrepreneurs and founding teams to The Innovation Hub for special events and networking opportunities. The only incubator of its kind in South Africa, eKasiLabs was founded in strategic support of the Township Economy Revitalization initiative, a provincial economy policy created to bolster the Gauteng economy. "The idea is to address entrepreneurship and innovation issues townships are facing," says Nothile Mpisi, the general manager of eKasiLabs.

For Nothile, who worked in enterprise development at the reputable incubator Raizcorp before joining The Innovation Hub in 2015, the main goal is to unlock the innovation potential of talented individuals and teams in townships. What's often holding these entrepreneurs back is a lack of access to vital entrepreneurial resources such as funding, new markets, infrastructure, prototyping facilities, mentorship and global alignment. On both the local and global scale, eKasiLabs fulfills The Innovation Hub's goal of fostering innovation all the while showing how vital it is for every ecosystem to bring innovation to emerging and indigenous knowledge-system markets. Bringing innovation development and support to townships positively impacts local and regional economies and sets an example on a global scale.

Nothile notes that there is an abundance of talent in townships, especially among the younger generations. Incubating entrepreneurship in townships empowers people to realize their innovative potential and boosts employment.

Most important tips for startups:

- **Ensure that your innovation fulfills an important need.** Research the issues underpinning your innovation as much as possible in order to understand the problem you're responding to and make sure that your innovation does, in fact, fulfill a regional and possibly global need.

- **Start local and then go global.** It's important to use innovation to address local needs. However, you should also seek to bring the innovation you develop in Gauteng to the rest of the world. Ask yourself whether your solutions can be used on a global scale.

- **Be collaborative in how you make a difference.** Not only should you seek to make a positive impact with your startup, you should also be willing (and even excited) to work with others in the entrepreneurial landscape. Networking is a key component to success, second only to giving back to your network.

"If we come closer to townships as an innovation center, we're bringing the opportunity for them to create their own employment and for the community as well," says Nothile. At the same time, the innovative ideas coming from townships are addressing really pressing needs, something all entrepreneurs should take note of. "These entrepreneurs and startups respond to social issues."

In addition to infrastructure support and thorough guidance, eKasiLabs aligns with universities, corporates and other organizations to play important, collaborative roles in the lives of entrepreneurs in the program. "We cannot do innovation and enterprise development alone," says Nothile. "It is very important that we align ourselves with stakeholders and partners who will assist these entrepreneurs." eKasiLabs leverages these connections to introduce its participants to potential customers and investors. Participants are emboldened to work with external stakeholders and even more so with their peers within the program. "We encourage the culture of collaboration and of cross-selling amongst each other," says Nothile. Startups should seek to be one another's customers and service providers. To encourage this environment of collaboration, eKasiLabs also plans networking events and summits.

Although much of what eKasiLabs does is to translate indigenous knowledge systems into market-ready innovation, the learnings are valuable to all entrepreneurs. Nothile's advice for township innovators is to allow the full product-development process to take shape and to not get married to one idea, instead opting for flexibility and willingness to learn in the face of changes. In addition, you should focus on capturing local markets before moving globally and not waste time once your product is ready for your first market, as competitors may just steal your great idea.

Founders from more established regions can learn a lot from township entrepreneurs and can gain new perspectives on topics such as the importance of impact. For townships, creating an innovative new startup is a matter of responding to community challenges, which is why many of the companies eKasiLabs produces are in social entrepreneurship. Entrepreneurs from all over should address problems that are really pressing in their communities and even see if their neighboring regions could benefit from access that's so easily taken for granted.

About

The Innovation Hub, established by the Gauteng Provincial Government through its Department of Economic Development, is an innovation agency that fosters economic development. eKasiLabs, one of its four incubators (the others being Maxum, Biopark and Climate Innovation Centre South Africa), specializes in entrepreneurial business development for townships in the Gauteng province, linking governmental, academic and corporate partners to entrepreneurs. With the goal of bringing innovation centers to townships, eKasiLabs offers services to enable and grow startups. These include skills development, networking opportunities and access to funding.

[Contact]   Email: nmpisi@theinnovationhub.com Telephone: +2712 844 000

[Links]   Web: theinnovationhub.com Facebook: InnovHubZA Twitter: @InnovHub

"*We encourage the culture of collaboration and of cross-selling amongst each other.*"

Shawn Theunissen / Property Point

Founder

Enterprise and Supplier Development

More than a decade ago, Shawn Theunissen founded Property Point because he was passionate about helping small businesses in South Africa – especially Black-owned businesses – overcome common challenges and tap into new opportunities in the market. "Our aim is to help develop businesses to the point where they're able to provide a value proposition and contribute positively to the economy," he says.

Property Point is an enterprise- and supplier-development program that was initially funded by Growthpoint Properties Limited, one of the largest South African real estate investment trusts listed on the Johannesburg Stock Exchange (JSE). To date, other funding partners include Attacq Properties, Fortress REIT Limited and the Small Enterprise Development Agency. At its core, Property Point is dedicated to unlocking opportunities for SMEs operating in South Africa's property sector. In addition to being the founder of Property Point, Shawn is also the Corporate Social Responsibility Executive at Growthpoint Properties.

Since Property Point's launch in 2008, over 170 businesses have graduated from its two-year accelerator program that helps participants scale their businesses into viable businesses. While developing the program early on, Shawn realized that many fledgling entrepreneurs faced not only business obstacles but also psychological barriers that stemmed from unconscious biases. "Working with small businesses is perceived to be high risk," he says. "If a business is small and Black-owned, the perceived risk is even higher. So the question was, 'How do we overcome these barriers and biases?'"

After much research on this topic, Shawn set up Property Point's accelerator program with the aim of reducing these barriers and fostering a business environment that enables burgeoning entrepreneurs to flourish. The resulting program revolves around the three Rs – risk, reputation and relationship – and how they impact the trajectory of a business. Basically, it focuses on helping participants to minimize the perception of risk that's associated with small businesses, develop a reputation that's based on a good track record, and build relationships with clients, staff and suppliers.

Most important tips for startups:

- **Define your target market.** Take some time to conduct research about your target customer. Consider what their needs might be and how your startup can solve these issues for them.

- **Understand your value proposition.** Think about what differentiates your product or service from what's already out there in this space. Figure out what you do better than your competitors and then clearly communicate your value proposition.

- **Make sure you have a clear business model.** While developing and implementing a successful business model is no easy feat, the main thing is to prioritize this task during the early stages. Having a business model in place will increase your chances of success.

In addition to that, Shawn and his team work closely with businesses to support them with business fundamentals such as getting their product or service market-ready, gaining insights on financial management, and developing processes that can optimize the functioning of a business. Even after graduating from their program, companies can turn to Property Point for further assistance, encouragement and support.

When asked about what advice he'd offer entrepreneurs looking to launch a sustainable small business in Johannesburg, Shawn shared some valuable insights with us: First, it's important to define your target market in order to pick up on the opportunities within a certain space. "Spend time doing the research to understand who your customer is, what their needs are and what problem you're solving for them," he says. Not only that, you must also thoroughly consider how this target market and their needs might evolve in the future.

Next, it's crucial to understand your value proposition and be able to communicate that clearly. Shawn suggests founders ask themselves these two questions: What makes my product or service unique? How is it better than what competitors are offering?

One way to ensure your company is on a path towards growth is by getting a clear idea about where your money is coming from. "Make sure you have a clear business model," says Shawn. While developing and implementing a successful business model is no easy feat, the main thing is to prioritize this task during the early stages.

Although Property Point's accelerator program caters predominantly to small businesses operating in the property sector, they have another offering that's sector-agnostic called Entrepreneurship to the Point (ettp.co.za), which Shawn describes as a series of networking sessions aimed at "informing, equipping and inspiring entrepreneurs" with tools and resources so they can reach their potential. Each month, a group of experts discusses a particular topic of interest, ranging from how to get funding for your business to the mental health of entrepreneurs.

About

Property Point is an enterprise- and supplier-development program that was initially funded by Growthpoint Properties Limited, one of the largest South African real estate investment trusts listed on the Johannesburg Stock Exchange (JSE). Established in 2008, Property Point has been a proud catalyst for successful enterprise and supplier development. Its carefully developed two-year program provides entrepreneurs with the skills, training and personal development support they need to develop their enterprises into fully independent companies.

[Contact]   Email: **info@propertypoint.org.za** Telephone: **010 593 4604**

[Links]   Web: **propertypoint.org.za** Facebook: **Proppoint** Twitter: **@PropPoint**

"Understand who your customer is, what their needs are, and what problem you are solving for them."

Cathy Smith and Kwena Mabotja / SAP

Managing Director, SAP Africa
Sub-Saharan Africa Director, SAP Next-Gen

[Sector]   **Enterprise Application Software**

"Johannesburg is the economic capital of South Africa," says Cathy Smith, managing director of SAP Africa. "There's a cosmopolitan and diverse population in the city that's growing at a rate of knots, so it's a rich environment for doing interesting new things, especially when it comes to using technology to solve problems in society or in business."

With technology advancing so quickly these days, there's a major need for young companies to enter the IT space and leave their mark. Cathy tells us that it's very important for SAP Africa to engage with local startups and support them in their journey of growth because it's part of the software giant's DNA to give back to the places in which they operate and to be able to share the wealth in those countries. For instance, SAP partners with Wits University's Tshimologong Precinct – a local digital innovation hub that offers incubator programs for entrepreneurs – to help transform startup ideas into viable businesses.

South Africa's largest city is going through rapid change, and this means that plenty of opportunities are opening up for startups and innovators across industries. While there's no lack of ideas or drive to innovate in Johannesburg, budding entrepreneurs still face challenges like getting access to funding to support later-stage growth or acquiring the business skills needed to get their startup to the next level.

"There's a high youth unemployment rate here as well as a big gap in terms of entrepreneurial and technical skills," says Kwena Mabotja, Sub-Saharan Africa director of SAP Next-Gen, a purpose-driven university and community enabling companies, partners and universities to innovate in connection with the seventeen UN Sustainable Development Goals (SDGs). "However, what's unique to Johannesburg is that many accelerators and incubators focus heavily on education and skills development. At SAP Next-Gen, we make a big effort to engage with both accelerators and the community to tap into opportunities that exist within the SAP ecosystem."

Most important tips for startups:

- **Link your startup to one of the UN Sustainable Development Goals.** In addition to making money, it's becoming increasingly important for entrepreneurs to tackle societal problems and work on solutions that will leave a positive impact on the world.

- **Once you have a viable idea, consider how it can become a solution that's relevant globally.** Being able to articulate how your idea will become a business that can expand across countries is a great way to attract investors.

- **Remember, technology isn't a means to an end.** Think about how tech can act as an enabler in your startup's growth.

To further support the local community, SAP launched its Skills for Africa Programme in Johannesburg, which provides participants with professional and technical training; and it recently teamed up with the Women in Data Science (WiDS) initiative in the city, which aims to empower women and girls to enter the world of science, technology, engineering and mathematics.

Both Cathy and Kwena believe that "glocalizing" is a critical aspect of SAP's overarching strategy. "Understanding the local context and giving back is important but we also need to remember to always stay in sync with what's happening globally since we're operating on the international stage as well," explains Cathy.

When asked to share their top pieces of advice for entrepreneurs starting up in Johannesburg, Kwena responded by saying it's important to find solutions to the big challenges in society. "Ask yourself how all these new technologies and business models can be applied to social issues and leave a positive impact," she says. "The UN SDGs are a good starting point."

Once you have an idea that tackles a relevant social issue, Cathy says, it's crucial to understand how it can become a global solution and to be able to articulate that to different audiences, such as potential investors. "Take your idea and find a way to turn it into a business that can expand across boundaries, because that's one way to get investors to pay attention," she says.

Last but not least, Kwena says, "Think about how technology plays a role as an enabler to get a scalable business."

About

SAP is the market leader in enterprise application software, helping companies of all sizes and industries run at their best. SAP Next-Gen is a purpose-driven innovation university and community aligned with SAP's commitment to the Sustainable Development Goals and supporting SAP's 437,000+ customers across 25 industries in 180+ countries. The community leverages 3,700+ educational institutions, 150+ SAP Next-Gen Labs and hubs at universities and partner and SAP locations, 160+ SAP Next-Gen Chapters, 25+ innovation communities through a partnership with Startup Guide, and a growing global network of 30+ FQ Lounges, the Home of Equality @ Campuses, in partnership with The Female Quotient.

[Contact]   Email: kwena.mabotja@sap.com Telephone: +27 (11) 235 6000

[Links]   Web: sap.com/africa Facebook: SAPAfrica Twitter: @SAPAfrica Instagram: SAP

"Ask yourself how all these new technologies and business models can be applied to social issues and leave a positive impact."

foun

ders

Beth Malatji

Founder / ReBeth Wines

Limpopo-born Beth Malatji began her business journey with the launch of *Wealth Ladder* magazine, an online publication focused on entrepreneurial success stories. She successfully exited the company and has now changed tack to run ReBeth Wines, which sources artisanal and organic coffee and wine products from traditional family farms for sale. As an author of *The Bootstrapper's Lifesaving Hacks*, a guide to bootstrapping, and as chapter director of Startup Grind Johannesburg, she's also a well-known face within the local entrepreneurial ecosystem.

What is your personal background?

I grew up in a small township in Limpopo, Seshego. I went to university but dropped out pretty quickly; I always just wanted to do my own thing. I'm fascinated by creating meaningful solutions. In the early days of my career, I was always faced with challenges that required me to step out of my comfort zone and create solutions. Entrepreneurship is all about solving problems. Creating a startup, or managing any business, is all about problem-solving too. So I founded *Wealth Ladder* magazine as my first venture.

What did the business do?

It was focused on business visibility, and it was for entrepreneurs. We wanted to tell inspirational success stories in an interactive way. Through that, I got involved in this entrepreneurial world. I just loved the energy of it all, the fact creative people were out there solving all sorts of problems. It was really very cool. I am fascinated by the idea of starting something from scratch and building all the way up.

How did you make it a success?

At the time I launched the magazine, I didn't really have a sense of direction or any real clue about how I was going to start, who was going to give me the support, and how we were going to grow. It was tough getting started. I didn't have money or connections, and I needed to automate as many things as possible within the business. I learned a lot about how to use free tools to get on and grow the business without lots of staff and money. It was such a valuable lesson that I wrote a book about it, *The Bootstrapper's Lifesaving Hacks*, to tell other entrepreneurs how to do the same.

Tell us about the exit from the magazine.

It had gone really well, but I was burnt out and wanted out. To tell the truth, it was harder than I thought it would be. I found myself working ten times harder than I should have been. Sometimes, you start something because you think you love it, but it's OK to let go and start something else. Before you mess it up, leave. I wanted something new and didn't want anything to do with media.

So you went into the wine industry? Tell us about the business.

I always wanted to have a product. ReBeth sources artisan, organic and biodynamic products from traditional family farms for sale to a wider market. Many of our products are hand-picked and crafted by local artisans. We want to bring to our customers' tables food that makes them feel lively, renewed, cheerful and connected, including wine, cheese and coffee collection. Basically, I love wine, and I love coffee. My belief is simple: you cannot sell anything if you do not have a love and passion for your own product. I have aspirations of owning a vineyard. This is just getting my foot in the door. This is level one.

How did you develop this business?

My business model got tweaked along the way, as we now assist other aspiring entrepreneurs who would like to get into the wine and coffee business. This time, I've really been helped by my mentor, who connected me with the right people to speak to. This helped me a lot, and I'd recommend getting mentored to any aspiring entrepreneur. Mentors have the potential to be very important for a small business. But entrepreneurs must be able to articulate their business in such a way that they're not wasting their mentors' time. Good mentors are very, very busy; they have their own things going on, so you need to use them wisely. You should keep it industry-specific, to ensure you're tapping into the right expertise. Otherwise, the best thing to do is to try business coaching. Make sure the information you want from the mentor is not something you could just Google.

How has it gone? What landmarks have you seen?

I'm learning as I go. Every day is a real learning curve for me. I discover something new about the industry every day, about how wine is made, that will tie in other elements of daily life. I think the trick is to surround myself with thought leaders from within my industry and to be as active as possible with everything that is happening. That's the best way to succeed. The truth is, building a business brings lots of unexpected twists – people quit, products fail, you burn out. It's not about getting it right the first time but getting it right eventually.

" *Your time is the greatest resource and one thing you can't get back. To execute at the top level, you have to understand the full gravity of time.* "

Where did you learn to hustle?

I think hustling is innate. I do not think it's something one learns. I would say that hustling is the result of wanting something to work out real bad. If you're so convicted in what you believe in, people will buy into your energy. But it goes beyond even this. Business models are the crucial ingredient of any startup. You need to look at a business model that you can articulate and that makes sense to you and your industry. My model has changed a lot from day one. If you see a gap in the market, go for it. Anything that makes sense for you, go for it.

What have your best entrepreneurial decisions been?

It took me some time, but I eventually realized that I cannot do everything by myself. So, with that in mind, the main one would be deciding to set up teams and systems within my business. This saves a lot of time and avoids a lot of confusion, and it frees you as a founder to focus on what is most important: strategizing, selling, and growing your business. If you try to do everything yourself, you will burn out. One other good decision was realizing that time is valuable and needs to be used wisely.. Your time is the greatest resource and one thing you can't get back. To execute at the top level, you have to understand the full gravity of time. It's imperative to prioritize your life and business in a way that lines up with what you value most.

What advice would you give to young entrepreneurs just starting out?

You need to educate yourself about the industry you're in. If you don't know it inside out, you are not going to succeed. Be obsessed about an industry leader, learn all the hacks and tricks, engross yourself within that sector. Whatever industry you're in, familiarize yourself with the main game players, go to events, learn from people. The other bit of advice would be very functional. Get your house in order, from legal to customer relationships. It sounds boring, but a good business is an organized business, with systems and transparency.

How did you come to be involved with Startup Grind, and what is its impact?

I first joined Startup Grind because I loved the local entrepreneurial space and wanted to get active within it. I used to run events, and there was a space to run Startup Grind in Jozi. Maybe it was meant to be for me. I love entrepreneurial ecosystems, and I love the energy, especially in Jozi. I love the diversity of the entrepreneurship ecosystem here. I am here as a go-to person for this type of stuff. It has been amazing; I've met some really cool entrepreneurs and business owners. It's really helped the other projects I'm involved in. Startup Grind has a big impact on entrepreneurs, mainly on networks and building startup communities that thrive together.

Why is Johannesburg a good place to start a business?

There is such a vibrant local entrepreneurial ecosystem here; I just love it. The diversity, the convenience, and the buzz. It is like any startup cannot afford to sleep. It's called "Johustleburg" for a reason. People leave all the other provinces of South Africa to come here and hustle. It is, and always has been, the city of gold. It is where all the opportunities are. There is every type of business here, every different culture, all different ways of doing things, really different energy levels. It is such an exciting space.

Are there any issues entrepreneurs face within the Johannesburg ecosystem?

It is quite decentralized, which can be challenging. If you go to Cape Town, you know the entrepreneurship scene will be at a specific place, but in Johannesburg, it's everywhere. This means it can be quite difficult to tap into, which is a big challenge. It can also be quite intimidating, as some of the big players within the ecosystem seem like they're not easy to reach unless you're introduced by someone. It can also be quite a divided city in a way. If you are an entrepreneur from Soweto, getting to Sandton might be a challenge. The language is different; the pace is different.

[About] **ReBeth** sources artisan, organic and biodynamic products from traditional family farms, with many of its products still hand-picked and crafted by local artisans in Africa. The company prides itself in the authenticity of its cheese, wine and coffee products.

[Links] Web: rebeth.co.za Facebook: rebethwines Twitter: @ReBeth__ Instagram: @rebeth__

What are your top work essentials?
Google Docs, because I can work on a file with
multiple people.

At what age did you found your company?
Twenty-six.

What's your most-used app?
Gmail.

**What's the most valuable piece of advice
you've been given?**
Learn as much as you can about the industry you're in.

What's your greatest skill?
Interpersonal skills.

Mpumelelo Mfula

Founder / RHTC Online Store

Gauteng-born and bred, Mpumelelo Mfula (popularly known as "Frypan") is a graduate of the University of the Witwatersrand and has been an entrepreneur from the start. Fresh out of his studies, he launched his first business, RHTC Online Store, to connect African streetwear brands with customers across the world, and he's since earned a reputation as one of the continent's most creative entrepreneurs. His latest venture is The Playground, which designs, manufactures and sells premium yet affordable furniture for modern entrepreneurs.

What are your earliest experiences of entrepreneurship?
I spent most of my upbringing in various parts of the East Rand of Gauteng province. I was that kid who sold sweets in primary school, and I got better at being the connect for little things my mates wanted at school but couldn't get at the tuck shop or at their favorite retail stores. I started, and then I doubled my investment of ten rand to twenty rand after selling out on the day. That moment changed my perspective on money. I couldn't understand why everyone wasn't doing this with their money and time. My relationship with making money has been good ever since.

To what extent did university prepare you for entrepreneurship?
I graduated at Wits University in 2012 with a bachelor's degree and an honors degree in political studies. The institution helped me develop a good work ethic and, most importantly, taught me about the value of commitment. Starting and finishing a degree is a great war with a number of battles, which is very similar to the journey of an entrepreneur. The social side of varsity inspired the hustler in me. I met some of the most impressive and artistic entrepreneurs on the Wits University lawns and at the parties and social spaces outside campus. These were the spaces which influenced and inspired my flair and creative approach to entrepreneurship.

How did you end up starting your own business?

After graduating in 2012, I was told that it takes an average of six months to get a job after graduating. I couldn't stay broke for that long, so I decided to live my politics and acted on an idea I'd had for a few months by creating an online store and network space exclusively for local streetwear entrepreneurs. This was my first formal business, and I called it RHTC, an acronym for "Returning Home To Create." Six months after launching, business was good and I'd found purpose in a community I cared about, so I dedicated more of myself to the development of youth entrepreneurs in South Africa while participating in business. This has given me an opportunity to establish a furniture retail company called The Playground, and Let's Play Outside, which is an agency that mainly works within the youth market space.

Why these types of businesses?

It just comes with the nature of being youthful. My ventures are based on solving problems that have personally posed as a challenge to my imagination as a youth and as an entrepreneur. Streetwear has been one of the most democratic spaces in South Africa for the youth in the last two decades. Access to the fashion industry is not as challenging as other industries for the youth, and we have found accessible and viable ways to design, customize and retail our products. The internet has also helped with the democratization of this space and allowed us to create a somewhat solid business community amongst ourselves as youth in business.

My second venture was inspired by not being able to afford rent at preferred areas for our offering, so I collaborated with friends to build a mobile and multifunctional stall for our popup tour in 2015. The stall was more popular than the clothes we were selling at certain spaces, so we decided to establish a furniture retail company that would design and produce mobile, multifunctional and affordable furniture, with the mission of encouraging youth entrepreneurship and making it more accessible to more people.

What landmarks have you seen?

When we organized two festivals in Johannesburg with a limited budget and with more than one hundred creatives as our main currency. The Let's Play Outside festival stands as the only festival independently organized by more than one hundred youth street artists in Johannesburg. We hosted the first festival in September 2017 and the second one in April 2018. Both involved young local creative entrepreneurs within the streetwear, social sports, visual culture and music space. Over three thousand young people attended the festivals.

The success of both was a manifestation of a long-term belief I had but couldn't articulate and give relevant reference to. The seasons of both festivals opened me up to the reality that there is a future for a Johannesburg and Africa that allows for youth participation. As to how it will look, that is up to us.

"The youth market is complex and very impressionable, yet they stand as the main players in driving trends and popular culture."

How viable are youth as a target market?

The youth market is complex and very impressionable, yet they stand as the main players in driving trends and popular culture. This makes the youth market an exciting community that encourages businesses to not only treat them as consumers but also to involve them in the story and, at times, in the operations of their business. That understanding informs our approach to our interaction with the youth market; we understand that they are the most valuable players both as partners and consumers.

What challenges and opportunities are there associated with running ecommerce businesses?

It's a growing market in South Africa, and the shift to the internet by traditional, corporate businesses and institutions has been a clear indication of the investment being made to train society to consume more online. This offers opportunities to developing entrepreneurs and businesses to leapfrog into modern and cheaper internet-based platforms to participate in business. However, the shortfall is the high data prices, which minimize the potential consumer reach and the opportunities for people to upskill and empower themselves using internet platforms. Every second South African uses a smartphone and uses the internet in some way – this shows potential to consume and use the internet for business. Lack of technical know-how and high data costs limit potential consumer reach and skilled contributors to the ecommerce space.

What have been your best decisions?

To stick to what I felt was the future of street culture even when I couldn't articulate it well enough to anyone, let alone to myself. I had to allow myself to develop as an entrepreneur to understand what it was that I was pursuing and the rules that inform the climate of the industry I was part of.

What have been your biggest mistakes?

An unbalanced relationship between executing my vision and finances. I had a season where I was too focused on executing my personal vision for projects we produced, and I neglected a great part of the health of the business's finance. The results were predictably unfortunate. That occasion taught me the value and importance of patience, discipline and focus in the game of entrepreneurship.

What advice would you give to entrepreneurs starting out?

Just start. You have to start somewhere to participate in the game of entrepreneurship. Start with what you have, and with the time you can afford to invest. Starting is the most important step. Also, focus on the bottom line. 2016 was one of my breakthrough seasons as a recognizable player in the youth space. I got a lot of credible press and speaking opportunities at popular platforms. I enjoyed the moment and planned on growing my popularity with the hopes that it would positively impact my business. A senior of mine invited me to his office and reminded me of my responsibility as an entrepreneur to create structures that will allow opportunities for other entrepreneurs. That served as a warning to not be lost in the hype and to focus on the bottom line and who I was and am.

Is it true that people are born to be entrepreneurs?

I wouldn't say it's true or false; however, what I know is that circumstances and conditions one grows up under do influence and spark interest to enter the entrepreneurship space. I, for one, grew up with my parents working under exploitative conditions at certain times when they had jobs. That experience informed my decision not to put my career and life fully in the hands of other people. My reaction was to use entrepreneurship as a political tool to bring justice to myself and those who share the same values and reality.

How have you funded your businesses? Is money out there?

My business and projects are self-funded. I believe that help is there through public and private institutions; however, there is a recognizable disconnect between funding opportunities, institutions and entrepreneurs on the ground. I believe that this will get better with time as the entrepreneurial culture grows within the youth community and when we have more prepared and committed youth in institutions that offer funding.

Why is Johannesburg a good place to start a business?

It's a vibrant city with some of the most diverse people from this continent and the rest of the world. The people carry the city's energy well, and it doesn't sleep. It's a youthful space. Joburg is one of the most developed cities in the continent of Africa, yet there is still a great amount of development and innovation that lies ahead of this city. This makes it an exciting terrain for any ambitious entrepreneur to play in.

[About]   RHTC Online Store is an ecommerce platform dedicated to marketing and distributing African-owned streetwear brands to an international market. Currently distributing thirteen leading African brands, RHTC has also hosted a number of workshops and events.

[Links]   Web: rhtconline.wordpress.com Facebook: RHTCstore Twitter: @RHTCOnline Instagram: rhtconline

What are your top work essentials?
My phone, my laptop and, most importantly, a smart team.

At what age did you found your company?
Twenty-three.

What's your most-used app?
WhatsApp, which I use for both personal and
business matters.

**What's the most valuable piece of advice
you've been given?**
To concentrate on the bottom line.

What's your greatest skill?
Connecting with people.

Musa Kalenga

Cofounder / Bridge Labs

Born in Zambia, Musa Kalenga is the cofounder and CEO of Bridge Labs, which builds technology products for entrepreneurs and small and medium-sized businesses, and strives to support "digital invisibles" and young black talent. A respected thought leader in the marketing industry, he is also the chief future officer at the House of Brave Group, where he advises on future-fit business strategy for organizations in a new digital world. Prior to entering the world of entrepreneurship, he was a client partner at Facebook and head of brand at IAB South Africa. As an event speaker and strategist, he has also been recognized as one of the "Top 200 young South Africans" by the *Mail & Guardian* newspaper.

Why did you leave the corporate world?

I believe I served my time. The corporate world was a controlled experiment for me. A big part of being a young entrepreneur is feeling like you have a major blind spot for "corporate" or "formal" business. I spent time exploring corporate to ascertain how big this blind spot was, and, in truth, it wasn't that big. So when I felt I'd given all the value I could and received all the value I could, I made the decision to leave and get back into my lane as an entrepreneur and value creator.

Tell us how you ended up starting your own business?

My first business was started in primary school – selling ice lollies after school to friends while walking home. It was purely opportunistic and made a lot of sense to me at the time. In between, I've had many businesses with varying degrees of success, but my current business, Bridge Labs, was born from a need to create a new kind of value equation in African technology.

What is Bridge Labs?

Bridge Labs is an engineering business; we are a collection of technologists as well as marketing people. The business model is about creating a whole technology product and being able to take it to market. We have our own products – an online education platform called Clock, and a second-hand car dealership CRM called Traction – but we also partner with external clients to build them products.

How did the idea come about?

When I was at Facebook, one of the things that inspired me – but also freaked me out and stressed me out a lot – was the sheer number of engineers available to look at any number of problems at any given moment. So when I left, the idea was to create an environment where we have many African engineers in one place, solving for African problems, and where we could actually think about anything, from any sector or industry, and be able to build a solution for it. So Bridge Labs has not focused on one particular industry, like adtech or fintech or edtech, but rather on being able to solve problems and deploy technology solutions quickly, and in so doing being able to play across a number of different industries quite easily.

Why launch this type of business?

The fourth industrial revolution requires a different kind of mindset and approach: it requires mathematics, science, problem solvers, and makers. As a technology business, we aim to bring these disciplines together to tackle some of Africa's most important challenges across various sectors. We deliberately chose not to specialize in a specific industry because our skills are universal and, as long as we believe in the problem we are solving, they can be used interchangeably.

Did your corporate experience prepare you for running your own business?

It gave me an appreciation of systems and process. It helped me start to appreciate what scale looks like and what it takes to achieve and maintain. It also helped me to understand how humans behave in organizations of such large populations.

How has it gone? What landmarks have you seen?

We have been blessed. In twenty-four months, we've launched four products in adtech, edtech, online retail and automotive. We've had some real failures along the way, but we now have a small but extremely capable core engineering team under the leadership of my cofounder Kolawole Olajide. We've been able to get some young, dedicated African talent into our business, so I'm happy from that perspective. We're starting to look at getting more diversity within our team, bringing a lot more female engineers and senior leaders into the business, which is something I'm quite excited about. We've also tried new models around commercialization and secured good partnerships with our clients. We made a modest profit in year one, and we've managed to substantially increase our revenue in year two without carrying any debt, so, from a financial perspective, I'm quite happy with our trajectory.

" *The fourth industrial revolution requires a different kind of mindset and approach: it requires mathematics, science, problem solvers, and makers.* "

What are your plans for the future?

It's just about us being able to stick to the plan. It is easy to veer off in all sorts of directions but so far we've stuck to the plan quite well. We're going to continue to scale our engineering capability. We have to double-down on the products we've already built. Clock has become a major focus now in terms of workplace learning and selling that into the market. We're also continuing to look at other strategic partnerships to add into our ecosystem, with the likes of IBM and big enterprise players, so we can not only upscale our engineering team but also understand how they can help us to build quicker and access slightly different capabilities at the enterprise level. We hope that we can continue building a really interesting space for young Africans – for young problem solvers – to come into and call home. So that's our plan, thinking about our value proposition to young engineers, mathematicians and marketers who want to get into the space. Defining that is something very important for us, to differentiate us as an employer.

Where did you learn to hustle?

I'm not sure I learned to hustle. I believe I was born with it, and I put myself in different contexts to refine my approach to the hustle. I also generally have other friends or references who have a unique and inspiring story of their own hustle, and we learn from each other.

What have been your best decisions and biggest mistakes?

My best decisions were leaving Facebook at the point that I did, partnering with Kola in the new venture, and always backing ourselves when faced with a crossroads. Often, you start businesses with people who have very similar skill sets to you, but those types of businesses tend to become quite frustrating quickly because there's no appreciation of mutual value. In terms of mistakes, at times we bite off more than we can chew, so we overextend ourselves. For people like me or Kola, we have the resilience and capability, but this is something we have to build into our teams, so a big mistake is not bringing them on the journey and supporting them adequately along the way.

Do you believe entrepreneurs get enough support?

Absolutely not. The kind of support that is available for entrepreneurs, unfortunately, tends to be quite weak, where you are effectively put into an incubator environment; you get free coffee and free wifi and some consultants you can speak to. While that environment solves one problem around infrastructure and support, it creates another, and that's an over-reliance. Part of being out in the wild and fighting for yourself and fending off wild animals is that you learn how to get some of those things paid for you, you learn how to generate revenue to get you over the line. So I think there's a real big red flag as far as incubators are concerned, because they create a bit of a crèche for startups. You don't get throughput, you don't get businesses coming through for a period of time and then leaving. The question is, how many of those businesses will list, sell or become successful?

Where would entrepreneurs benefit from more help?

The support required for entrepreneurs is around getting access to customers. Entrepreneurs are building products, they are innovating and doing all these crazy things, but they need access to markets. If you can put them in front of customers that are willing to pay for their services, that's the kind of support entrepreneurs need in order to thrive. There are one or two examples of how it is being done well, but I don't think it has been done on a wholesale level as it should. That's a big gap as far as supporting entrepreneurs goes.

What advice would you give to entrepreneurs starting out?

Just start. That's the best advice you'll ever receive. At no point will you have all the answers or all the boxes ticked, but you have to just start.

Why is Johannesburg a good place to start?

There's an increasing number of shared workplace environments with all the facilities you need, and there's a decent base of clients you can mine by being in the right environments. The cost of operating is moderate, depending where you set up, but it can be managed very well. And you have access to services providers – HR, finance, design, etc. – that have flexible engagement terms.

[About]   Bridge Labs is an engineering business – a collection of technologists and marketing people building solutions for external clients as well as building its own products, which include online-education platform Clock and used car dealership CRM Traction.

What are your top work essentials?
Notebook, laptop, binaural beats playlist and headphones.

At what age did you found your company?
My first company when I was nineteen,
Bridge Labs when I was thirty-one.

What's your most-used app?
WhatsApp, Asana and Outlook.

**What's the most valuable piece of advice
you've been given?**
Just start.

What's your greatest skill?
My ability to make authentic connections
with people of all creeds.

Palesa Sibeko and Vincent Hofmann

Cofounders, Directors / SiGNL

Palesa Sibeko and Vincent Hofmann immediately connected over their love of technology and creative design, and in 2011 they founded the digital consultancy Inquisition (now a work-design company called BetterWork). However, they began to realize their interest in building collaborative communities via tech wasn't being completely served by just one company. Creating the separate entity SiGNL in 2015 happened organically as Palesa and Vincent explored the boundaries of IoT and creative experiences. As all of their projects needed some level of interactivity, they brought on technician Tom van den Bon, who had a background in computer science and development, to bring their projects to life as their chief engineer and creative technologist. Together, the three have tackled all kinds of design challenges, such as interactive vending machines and museums of the future.

How did you come up with the idea for the company?

Vincent: SiGNL was founded as an entity alongside Inquisition. In a lot of our previous work, we weren't able to pursue the technology interests that we once had. We wanted to do business design and industrial design out of one firm, and what we were finding is that most South African clients were really reluctant to believe that we could do both. We had to set up SiGNL as a purpose vehicle to pursue our technology interests. What was quite interesting is that it liberated us from thinking like a traditional design firm. The three of us organically set up something that would allow us to pursue this project in a cooperative way.

Can you talk about some of the challenges you've faced and how you've overcome them?

Palesa: I think we didn't fit into the neat boxes people were really used to. We had to be understood for the value we could bring to people, and we actually cared about the impact of what we built. People tended to ask us to build custom hardware without knowing that a lot of things could go wrong without being given time and freedom for extensive development and testing. Even though clients were excited at the prospect of us building something one hundred percent to their specs, their risk appetite was extremely low. They wanted to treat it like an off-the-shelf project, which indicated a misunderstanding of R&D and customization.

Vincent: One of the biggest challenges to conducting R&D in Africa is the implicit costs of doing R&D aren't necessarily obvious to clients. The resolution to that problem is that we're having to absorb the cost of educating our clients as to what design really is before pursuing work with them. Because we come from the space of imagination, people presume that whatever they dream up is possible. One of the challenges is that people concoct crazy ideas and hope that we can build them, without realizing that the gap between idea and delivery means there has to be time and someone has to get paid.

Palesa: Sometimes when you're trying to help clients solve the core problem, they immediately want to jump to technology solutions, and we tell them no, we actually have to really understand what the problem is. You may not need to build anything at all. They just hear all these sexy things from places like Singularity University and so forth that may not be practical or relevant to their context.

What do you think has been your biggest mistake so far?
Vincent: The biggest mistake, I think, was letting our curiosity override our business strategy. If you looked at our body of work at the beginning, you'd probably find it was all over the place. The biggest thing we've learned is to keep things a bit more simple and coherent so that our clients and the people who consume our technology can understand the intent of our business.

Palesa: At some level, curiosity and excitement worked in our favor, in that we've exposed ourselves to experiences we normally wouldn't have by saying yes to things with ridiculous deadlines. Even when we're happy with the outcome, we think about what else we could have started instead of killing ourselves on just one project.

Vincent: One of the biggest mistakes we made early on was saying our time was cheap and our curiosity and passion for the work were fulfilling enough to undercharge and try to overdeliver. It diminishes your relationship with your client when you seem so excited you're willing to say yes to damn near anything. It certainly did come with a lot of learning, but it took us almost a year to rebound from all our yeses.

What do you believe has been your best decision?
Palesa: I'd say bringing on the people that we work with. I think we've been super lucky in that we've had people who have a great appetite for learning almost anything the project requires and who are willing to put in the work. Getting Tom on board was a great decision. His tremendous skill set and network has been very helpful for us.

"The most profound thing people can do is put their ideas out into the world."

Vincent: I think our approach to intellectual property. We've always looked to the open-source and maker movements for their ethics and policies toward making things. Because of that, I think one of our best ideas was this idea of not being a traditional company. We've always had very low walls around us and been super transparent about how our business works and how we are remunerated, and I think because of those things, we've had people who work with us give up more of their time and energy than they would for a normal, more traditional, profit-motivated company.

If you'd known more when starting out, are there things you would have done differently?
Palesa: I think we would focus a lot earlier. We were all over the place, accepting things purely out of interest. I think we've honed in on what we find to be quite valuable to us now, both from a profit perspective and also for our goal of having a social impact. We want to improve how people create and learn together in workplaces and schools, creating kickass hardware along the way.

Vincent: Treating ourselves less as imposters and being more courageous about what design can do in Africa. We could have focused and put up with slower growth of the business and a smaller body of work, but I think we would have been in a better place to say we could pursue a focus in R&D.

What advice would you like to give younger, less experienced entrepreneurs?
Vincent: Focusing on understanding how people are going to use your technology is way more important than what you end up building. Are we building to aid machines in their ultimate dominance of us, or are we building to improve and augment the way people live? I think if we were to give advice to young people, it would be to do the latter – it's something a lot of young engineers need to understand. Maybe pick up some humanities courses along your way because you'll have a limited view of what technology can do if you don't understand things in context. Almost all of our work values humans over technology.

Palesa: I agree with Vince: technology is just a tool. Of course, the technology needs to live up to the problem you're trying to solve.

Also, entrepreneurship is really hard. I hate it when entrepreneurship is presented as an attractive escape from the nine-to-five slog without also highlighting the trade-offs you have to make. It should be an avenue for you to make an impact on the world. So I would say that entrepreneurs shouldn't just sit quietly in their own basement trying to make things. Go out and see who else in the ecosystem can complement the work you're doing.

Vincent: In the world of ideas, you become very selfish about who you share with because you believe you're on to the next big thing. A lot of people impose limits on the impact their ideas can have because they don't want to share them with anyone. The most profound thing people can do is put their ideas out into the world. It's rule one of modern design: to validate your assumption by putting it out into the world.

Can you talk about the experience, and the pros and cons of starting up in Johannesburg?
Palesa: Right now in Joburg, we have a healthy startup scene. I feel that there's a lot of frustration and many obstacles, but people are still willing to go and do it, meaning that there's hope and resilience in the ecosystem. It's not nearly as fast or as rich as it could be, but I still think we're moving closer to a better situation in that sense, with people developing true innovations.

Vincent: When you're politically unstable, the appetite for risk and newness really does get diminished. People are turning to innovation and to young designers to tackle some of the social challenges that our state doesn't want to address. On the backside of this instability is that there's been a larger focus on what design can do to improve the way we live here in the African context with the scarcity of resources. That's the ecosystem we operate in. It's quite liberating once you know that there's no shortage of challenges. For us, the excitement, from a design perspective, is addressing some of the social challenges here. We've got privileged access to doing the good stuff.

[About]   SiGNL combines tailor-made software and hardware, and human-experience design, in building physical interactive systems inspired by the Maker Movement. The company has brought their interactive experiences to market leaders in many sectors, such as designing museums of the future for their clients. SiGNL's design philosophy is human-centered so that hardware and software can be leveraged to give greater meaning to data, events and experiences.

[Links]   Web: signl.co.za Twitter: @SiGNLLabs Instagram: SiGNLLabs

What are your top work essentials?
Palesa: Music and interaction with colleagues
(knowledge sharing).
Vincent: Running, cycling, my phone.

At what age did you found your company?
Palesa: Thirty-four.
Vincent: Thirty-three.

What's your most-used app?
Palesa: Audible, Pocketcasts, Waze.
Vincent: Strava, Pocketcasts, Medium.

**What's the most valuable piece of advice
you've been given?**
Vincent: You need to understand yourself and where
you can add value. Be more coherent.

What's your greatest skill?
Palesa: Diversity of thought based on different experiences.
Breaking boundaries and exploring design.

Sinenhlanhla Ndlela

CEO / Yococo

Sinenhlanhla Ndlela studied TV writing and post-production at university but ended up taking a very different path. After brief stints working as a photographer and a production assistant, she is now a "foodpreneur." In 2016, she founded Yococo, which produces and sells dairy-free ice cream, and now she says she's "serving love." The company has grown at a fast pace. It's currently available in Cape Town, Durban and Johannesburg, and Sinenhlanhla is planning to take it across South Africa and into international markets.

Tell us about your background.

I grew up between the Free State, KZN, Johannesburg and Cape Town, and went to university to study TV writing and post-production. I moved to Johannesburg full time after finishing my degree, as it was my intention at that time to complete my honors degree while also working part-time at a production company. But when I moved to Johannesburg I changed my mind about doing my honors, and so immediately started working full time instead. I worked in production for a while and was also a published freelance photographer, but I just did not feel fulfilled at all. I felt I had more to offer in terms of my contribution to the world and what I did with my time. I just did not see myself waking up every day to go to a job that I didn't quite enjoy. So I started to think about doing my own thing.

Why ice cream?

At around that time, I was really trying to figure myself out in terms of my purpose and why I'm here, basically. And I honestly really, really love ice cream! For me, it was the go-to thing. If ever I'm going to do something that makes me happy, it has to be to do with food or ice cream. It wasn't about money or ambition; it was just that I discovered what my purpose was: to serve love. It was also at a time when I was transitioning into a dairy-free lifestyle, and there just wasn't an ice cream that I particularly enjoyed. That's why I ended up doing this. I make the ice cream myself. I initially started out making yoghurt but switched as I thought maybe I wasn't being ambitious enough.

How has it been received?

It's gone really well. People love it, and we're now available in three cities. I've worked with big companies, and I've been asked to work with government departments. I've met a lot of great people, and we supply a lot of stores that are a really big deal. The whole journey has been really exciting.

How did you fund the business?

I've never really had any funding. It has just been from family, friends and my own savings. It's worked out just fine. I think funding can be important depending on what you're doing, but I don't think it should ever be the thing that stops you from starting. You really don't need funding to start a business. You need funding to grow, and I think it definitely helps your business escalate at a quicker rate. Funding can help, but also it takes away from learning your business inside and out, which is really important for any entrepreneur to do. If you get funding, you're going to miss so many steps.

Do you have any tips for founders planning to bootstrap their businesses?

You can just start small. I started really, really small, from my own place. I didn't start with what you'd think I would have needed, like a big kitchen or lots of big equipment. I just started working with what I had, and I really think it's better that way. At the end of the day, your customers are the ones who help you build up your business. The more they want your product, the more they're going to buy from you, and the more of your product you can start making and selling. And then you can save money from there. You should start with the end in mind, but you don't have to go big from the start. If you don't have to buy things, don't buy them. You don't have to have an office space; you can just use your home at the start—as long as you're producing your product. Don't do things to make yourself look big for other people. If your product doesn't need certain things, certain facilities, then don't start there; start small.

What does the future look like for Yococo?

We're pretty ambitious. I want to employ many more people, of course, and I want to see us in many more shops. We're available in a handful of cities right now, but I want to see us have a physical presence in the main cities across South Africa and also eventually go international. Everyone loves ice cream, and our product is filling a really important gap for people.

Where does your entrepreneurial spirit come from?

Believe it or not, I didn't always want to be an entrepreneur. I never actually thought I'd be one myself. Both of my parents are entrepreneurs, and I used to see the struggles they would go through, the problems they had to face, and think I didn't want something like that for myself. I also never wanted to be in a position where I was leading people, yet I have always ended up in positions where I am, even if it's not in traditional ways. I guess I get it from my parents. My mum is really a hustler, she could make literally anything happen. All the women in my family are very strong and really driven. That's something I've always seen growing up. It was part of my upbringing more than anything.

" *You mustn't just get into a business for the sake of doing it. Entrepreneurs are meant to solve problems.* "

What has been your best decision?

I think it was definitely believing in myself from the beginning and quitting my job to start this business and do something I loved doing every day. Now I feel like it's become something bigger than me, and I really do believe I'm making a difference in my everyday life now. So that was an amazing decision, I believe.

Also, the people I chose to embark on this journey with me, my team at Yococo, is another great decision. They are the right people for the job, and they make me and the business stronger. Aside from it being part of my journey and part of my purpose, there was also a gap in the market for something like this, so it isn't just something that's for me alone.

Any major mistakes along the way?

In the same way that my best decision was starting on this journey in the first place, I guess my biggest mistakes were not believing in myself soon enough. At the very beginning of my journey, I also made a number of decisions from a place of desperation, which is never a very good idea.

How would you describe your experience of running a South African business as a female, black founder?

Right now, I think entrepreneurship is in the spotlight a lot, and there are a lot of people wanting to get involved, especially young black women, so that's really great. I think we're at a great time in terms of technology, we have access to so much information, and there are activations, a lot of avenues for us to look for information, which is really amazing. Yet there are still problems. The thing that I struggle with, in terms of racism, is if I need to get my product onto different shelves in different places that are still very backwards. Sometimes I do think that if I'd been from a more privileged background, perhaps I wouldn't experience that, and there wouldn't be so many blocks. And there are a lot of blocks, solely based on my gender and my race.

How much support is out there?

There are a lot of opportunities available to people currently, all sorts of accelerators and incubators, stuff like that. I myself have benefitted from mentors and incubators in running my business, and the support can be really valuable. But it doesn't just come from formal programs and initiatives. You can get that kind of support on an ongoing basis. There are a lot of things that I didn't know, and a lot of things that I still don't know. I'm still learning all the time. I surround myself with people who know more than me, and that's a really important thing to do.

What advice would you give to young entrepreneurs?

The key thing is to just believe in your product. If you have done your research, you know what your business is about, and you know why you're doing it. Entrepreneurship is getting very glamorized right now; it's a trendy thing that's happening, but you mustn't just get into a business for the sake of doing it. Entrepreneurs are meant to solve problems, and if you're not solving a problem and you're not making money, then you don't really have a business.

Why is Johannesburg a good place to run a business?

Jozi is a really great place to be because everything here happens fast – everything is moving at speed. There are a lot of people who are movers and shakers in different areas here, which means you have greater access to meeting people who can actually propel you to the next level. Things are just happening in Johannesburg.

[About] Yococo is a manufacturer of dairy-free ice cream that is available online and in retailers across South Africa.

[Links]   Web: yococo.co.za Facebook: theyococo Twitter: @the_yococo Instagram: the_yococo

What are your top work essentials?
Laptop, mango strips and a notebook.

At what age did you found your company?
Twenty-three.

What's your most-used app?
I have to say Instagram.

**What's the most valuable piece of advice
you've been given?**
Everyone started somewhere, so do the best with what
you know now, and when you know better, do better.

What's your greatest skill?
I am a problem solver.

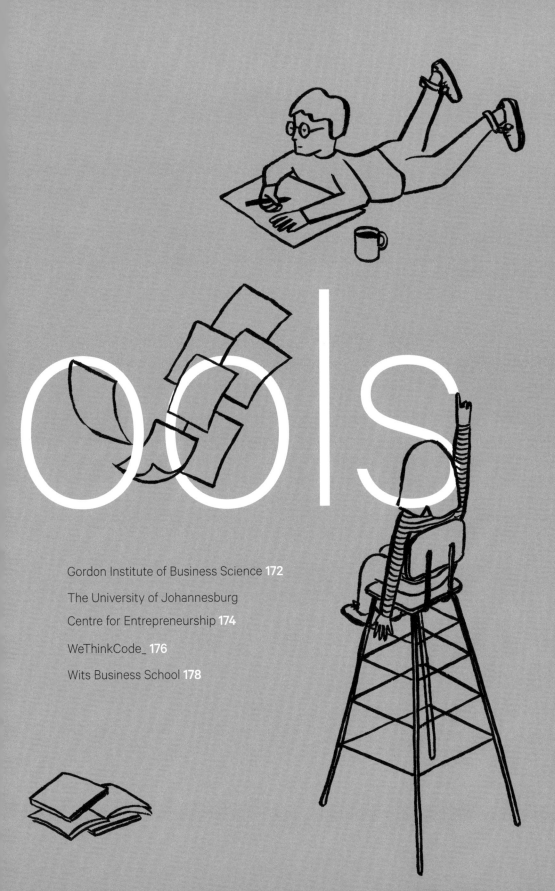

ools

- **Have a compelling idea.**
  You should have a strong idea of what positive change you want to bring about and be ready to develop solutions to do so.

- **Show you are teachable.**
  We look for people with the willingness to learn and challenge their assumptions.

- **Be passionate.**
  Entrepreneurship is about passion. We're looking for individuals with the desire to effect change and build businesses.

- **Be ready to grow.**
  Participants should already be running a social enterprise and be ready to scale their business into new markets or verticals.

[Name]
Gordon Institute of Business Science

[Elevator Pitch]
"We provide entrepreneurial leaders with the skills, tools and resources needed to build and run effective social enterprises."

[Enrollment]
60 students per year

[Description]
Founded in 2000, the University of Pretoria's Gordon Institute of Business Science (GIBS) is an internationally accredited business school. Its entrepreneurship-focused unit, the GIBS Entrepreneur Development Academy (EDA), partners with institutions and works with entrepreneurs in both the formal and informal sectors at various phases of their business development. Its range of programs are developed based on research into what really works for entrepreneurial development, and they make use of innovative teaching and learning techniques. "As a result, our programs have demonstrated significant impact in terms of business growth and job creation for over three thousand businesses since the EDA was established," says senior lecturer Kerrin Myres.

The EDA's flagship course is the Social Entrepreneurship Programme, a middle-management training program for people who want to make a difference. The year-long course, which takes excellence in business thinking and applies it to the social development space, is designed to provide social changemakers and entrepreneurs with the skills, creative thinking and networks needed to tackle complex social and economic issues. "It's aimed at those wanting to make a difference," says Kerrin. "Classes provide both a platform for passionate debate and a space where the diverse worlds of entrepreneurs, NGOs, business and government meet."

The program, which costs 36,000 ZAR ($2,500), is aimed at both local and international students and takes place in three four-day modules. Each module consists of theory (reading and lectures), context (case studies and guest speakers) and integration (syndicate work, assignments and projects), and participants are constantly assessed. The program covers the whole process of developing and growing a social enterprise, with subjects such as strategy, scaling, social change, marketing, financial management, governance and legal framework, and alternative income streams. "It helps participants to build personal and enterprise effectiveness that makes a difference in the businesses in which they operate," says Kerrin.

[Apply to]
gibs.co.za/about-us/centres/leadership_and_dialogue/social_entrepreneurship_programme

[Links]
Web: **gibs.co.za** Facebook: **GIBSsa** Twitter: **@GIBS_SA** Instagram: **gibsbusinessschool**

- **Show product-market fit.**
  You need to have an existing market and a strong understanding of it.

- **Be teachable.**
  We look for students that are not only receptive to learning but have an attitude that seeks to learn.

- **Show networking skills.**
  You must have the ability to network to reach the relevant connections.

- **Challenge your assumptions.**
  Entrepreneurs should be open to new ideas, be willing to adjust, be malleable, and be hungry for knowledge.

- **Show determination.**
  You must have determination, be passionate, and have tenacity.

[Name]

The University of Johannesburg Centre for Entrepreneurship

[Elevator Pitch]

"We are an outreach center aimed at fostering the next generation of entrepreneurs by teaching them the relevant skills and connecting them with markets and mentors."

[Enrollment]

400 per year

[Description]

The University of Johannesburg Centre for Entrepreneurship (UJCfE) is an outreach organization aimed at facilitating business development in townships and rural areas. It was formed in 2006 as a result of the University of Johannesburg's goal to be an international tertiary institution of choice in Africa and is recognized for its excellence in research, innovation, knowledge-building and collaboration. This hub for entrepreneurs, students, partners and investors aims to help create jobs and alleviate poverty. The center dedicates itself to providing the best in entrepreneurship education by developing and supporting a new breed of future-fit entrepreneurs. Director Moipone Molotsi says that it "fosters a culture of entrepreneurship among students and entrepreneurs at large, challenging the entrepreneurship landscape with thought leadership and innovation."

The center is funded by sponsors such as the Raymond Ackerman Academy, the Thebe Foundation and Shell Downstream South Africa, among others. It offers a host of programs, including the Raymond Ackerman Academy Program (designed for idea-phase businesses) and the Small Business Enrichment Programme (for more established SMEs). There are also more focused programs looking at topics such as financial management, socio-economic development and advanced social entrepreneurship, and an accelerator program for established startups. The programs range between 3,900 ZAR ($270) and 20,000 ZAR ($1,400) and are open to all students.

Moipone says that the UJCfE has built a solid ecosystem designed for long-term support to entrepreneurs, linking them to market-access opportunities within its partner ecosystem, which is manifested in its Integrated Business Development Model. Built on eleven key strategic elements, including innovative programs, entrepreneurship training, mentorship and IP commercialization, it has seen the center establish expertise in helping to develop township enterprises. "We have recently expanded our expertise to developing entrepreneurs' enterprises to be supplier-chain ready and inculcated a culture of entrepreneurship within the student community to encourage student startups even before they graduate," says Moipone.

[Apply to]

uj.ac.za/faculties/cbe/ujcfe

[Links]

Web: **uj.ac.za/faculties/cbe/ujcfe** Twitter: **@ UJCfE** LinkedIn: **school/uc-centre-for-entrepreneurship**

- **Demonstrate natural aptitude for learning.**
  Prove you have what it takes via our online bootcamps and see if you are #BornToCode by playing our online application games.

- **Work and thrive in a peer-to-peer learning environment.**
  If you work well with others, you will likely be a good fit.

- **Demonstrate that you are ambitious and a self-starter.**
  If you take initiative, have strong time-management skills and are committed to getting the most out of the WeThinkCode_ opportunity, we are looking for you!

- **Shine during our Selection Bootcamp.**
  Demonstrate your grit and resilience during our intense 3.5-week bootcamp.

WeThinkCode_

[Name]

[Elevator Pitch] *"We're a network of revolutionary tech institutions dedicated to delivering Africa's human potential and meeting the increasing demand for software-engineering skills by training the next generation of software developers."*

[Enrollment] **300 per year**

[Description] In 2016, Arlene Mulder and Camille Agon launched their school, WeThinkCode_, after a dinner conversation about digital skills – or lack of them. The school has been a revelation with its adoption of international models in a South African context. The nonprofit has since expanded to Cape Town and has plans to move into a host of other African markets. WeThinkCode_ partners with corporates to offer students free tuition in modern and relevant digital skills to help them enter the job market. Other partners provide the materials and support, such as a key deal with the Paris and Silicon Valley based Ecole 42. "We have no teachers or classes, and we use the most up-to-date methods of teaching people the most up-to-date skills," says Dylan Richts, head of partnerships at WeThinkCode_.

Students learn through peer-to-peer problem-solving, correcting each other's work and moving together through the program, a process that results in WeThinkCode_ graduates thinking slightly differently than at other schools. "WeThinkCode_, at its core, is dedicated to sourcing and placing excluded youth, who would otherwise not have an opportunity to participate in this skills-sparse sector," says Dylan. "This is particularly important given that the organization has developed in the South African context, where around fifty-two percent of young people are unemployed."

There are more than four hundred students across South Africa now undergoing the fully sponsored, two-year, full-time courses offered by WeThinkCode_, giving them the opportunity to move directly into employment. The same corporates that sponsor students to go through the program also offer them two internship opportunities of four months and potential routes into full-time employment upon completion of the program. "These opportunities to work with our corporate partners mean our students are better prepared than most to become valuable members of teams – and even founders of businesses – in the future," says Dylan. "We want to be the organization that bridges the gap between academia and business."

[Apply to] apply.wethinkcode.co.za/users/sign_up

[Links] Web: **wethinkcode.co.za** Facebook: **wethinkcode** Twitter: **@wethinkcode** Instagram: **wethinkcode**

- **Be proactive.**
  Students should be adaptive and show
  high levels of perseverance.

- **Be innovative and open-minded.**
  We are looking for people that can challenge
  their own assumptions and look at the world
  in a different way.

- **Have a degree.**
  You should preferably have an honors degree,
  but a first-class bachelor's degree together with
  a recognized and accredited postgraduate degree
  or diploma from any discipline is also acceptable.

- **Show your real-life experience.**
  Post-university entrepreneurial, corporate
  or informal business experience is an advantage.

Wits Business School

[Name]

[Elevator Pitch]
"We are one of the leading business schools in Africa, offering a variety of postgraduate academic and executive education programs to equip leaders for their future careers in entrepreneurship or the corporate world."

[Enrollment]
1,771 (2019)

[Description]
At the heart of the University of the Witwatersrand (Wits), one of the highest rated research universities in the world, stands the Wits Business School (WBS). Established in 1968, WBS has major international connections. It is accredited by the London-based Association of MBAs (AMBA) and is the only African business school to be a member of the Partnership in International Management (PIM), a network of sixty leading business schools around the world. "We are consistently rated as one of South Africa's best business schools and boast the highest number of PhDs among its faculty of any business school in South Africa," says Boris Urban, professor of entrepreneurship at WBS.

The school's expertise is built on its research output, which is the highest of any business school in South Africa, and its case studies. It was the first business school in South Africa to establish its own case centre, where it has developed well over 250 case studies, most of which focus on South African and African organizations. "The case method enriches the learning experience by bringing real-life scenarios into the classroom," says Boris. All of this attracts a mixture of both local and international students, with past students including CEOs, SME consultants, academics, entrepreneurs, venture capitalists, scientists, professionals and artists. 2019 fees are approximately 140,000 ZAR ($9,800).

WBS offers a one-year Master of Management in the field of Entrepreneurship and New Venture Creation (with a strong focus on research) for students focused on launching their own ventures. Its curriculum presents a holistic, integrated and multidisciplinary view of entrepreneurship, with students gaining a broad appreciation of entrepreneurial activities in a wide range of contexts, including technopreneurship, corporate entrepreneurship, social entrepreneurship and enterprise development. "It allows students to complement their general education while developing their entrepreneurial competencies," says Boris. "It exposes students to the latest and best research available on various aspects of entrepreneurship, which helps to dispel the many myths that exist in the popular literature surrounding entrepreneurship."

[Apply to]
wits.ac.za/postgraduate/applications

[Links]
Web: **wbs.ac.za** Facebook: **Wits.Business.School** Twitter: **@witsbschool**

inve

stors

- **Build a good team.**
Your team should have the ability to execute, incorporating the relevant technical skills, industry knowledge, professional networks and passion for the business.

- **Demonstrate a product-market fit.**
You should have identified a real problem in a growing market that your product or solution can solve in an innovative way.

- **Prove traction.**
You need to show us that you've signed up paying customers and generated revenue.

- **Have potential for scale.**
For early-stage investors such as ourselves, scalability is very important, so the growth prospects of the business need to be significant.

- **Have an exit strategy.**
It is vital that there are clear exit opportunities for the business and that investors will see a sizeable return on investment.

[Name] # Edge Growth

[Elevator Pitch] *"We channel corporate ESD (enterprise and supplier development) budget to SMEs by providing them with access to finance, markets and skills to grow their businesses and create economic impact."*

[Sector] **Finance, insurance, IT, healthcare, logistics, services, manufacturing, retail, energy**

[Description] Founded in 2007, Edge Growth was formed to make a tangible difference to the South African economy, alleviating poverty through job creation. The route it chose to achieve this was through partnering with corporates, and FirstRand Bank was the first to buy into this vision, seeding Edge Growth's first fund for growing SMEs with 86 million ZAR ($6 million). With the advent of the B-BBEE Codes of Good Practice, Edge Growth saw an opportunity to catapult its job-creation agenda by utilizing corporate funds to grow SMEs. "We're specialists in growing SMEs and creating impact beyond the benchmark," says Amina Patterson, the company's head of business development.

Edge Growth has worked with more than one hundred corporates, associations and investors and has 1.2 billion ZAR ($84 million) in assets under management. It has made a total of sixty-eight investments across fourteen sectors, with its average ticket size at 7.2 million ZAR ($500,000), and it has overseen twenty-two exits in the last eight years and created almost three thousand jobs. "Our seventy-five full-time employees are passionate about building a brighter future for our nation," says Amina. "Their collective inputs over the years have helped us evolve our purpose to include growing and building businesses to achieve job creation, Black wealth creation, transformation, socio-economic development and the deployment of entrepreneurial capital."

Edge Growth's clients are large commercial organizations in urban areas with ESD budgets of preferably 50 million ZAR ($3.5 million) and above. It seeks SMEs that are looking for three crucial advantages: funding, access to markets and the development of business capabilities offered through its acceleration programs. Edge Growth is approached on a daily basis by applicants for funding, says Amina, and it also sources investable SMEs through networking opportunities. "We want to work with corporates, associations and investors that share our vision and want to get involved in our groundbreaking programs and funds."

[Apply to] info@edgegrowth.com

[Links] Web: **edgegrowth.com** Facebook: EdgeGrowthSA Twitter: @Edge_Growth

- **Have a strong team.**
  The most important consideration is that the team has the ability to execute, with the right technical skills, passion, industry knowledge and relevant professional networks.

- **Demonstrate how your solution is unique.**
  Your solution needs to be innovative and be different from other solutions in the market. Any intellectual property is a bonus.

- **Show your potential to scale.**
  Your system should be able to cope with a broad customer footprint, and your solution should be able to take advantage of economies of scale. You should be solving an important problem or unmet need.

- **Have proven traction.**
  Having customers and revenue on the books always makes for an easier conversation, as knowing that people are willing to part with their money for the solution is a big win.

- **Be a good fit.**
  Entrepreneurs need to fit with the investor's mandate or preference, as investors prefer to invest in sectors they know and in markets in which they can move the dial.

Jozi Angels

[Name]

[Elevator Pitch] *"We're a group of angel investors who invest as individuals and syndicates in scalable, early-stage startups from Johannesburg and elsewhere in South Africa."*

[Sector] **Sector agnostic**

[Description] The idea for what is now angel investment group Jozi Angels initially took shape in 2014, when founder Abu Cassim, whose family owns an eighty-year-old Johannesburg-based textiles business, assisted local investors in backing a handful of early-stage Johannesburg businesses. This project was successful and, in 2017, it became a formal endeavor. The group now includes twenty-four investors who have made a combined thirty-six investments. It has also affiliated itself with larger investment groups, such as the South African Business Angel Network (SABAN) and the African Business Angel Network (ABAN). "We are not a fund but rather make investments in startups as individuals or syndicates," says Abu.

Once they have injected capital, Jozi Angels members become direct shareholders in the businesses they have funded, and members of the group are mostly successful entrepreneurs in their own right. Their varied expertise and experiences mean that Jozi Angels is sector agnostic. Funding has been obtained by startups as diverse as fitness solution FitKey, edtech offering Hippocampus and experience-booking platform Tour 2.0, with Abu stressing it is up to members where they put their money. "Each individual angel has his or her own investment preferences. We typically invest in scalable solutions that will attract follow-on funding from VCs and impact investors."

It's not just money that the group brings to the table but also knowledge and networks, and Abu says these are actually more valuable than capital. Startups should not expect a silent partner, as angels de-risk their investments by getting hands-on involved in the business. Jozi Angels aims to grow the network to fifty angels over the course of 2019 and increase deal flow in Johannesburg, which Abu considers one of the top tech hubs in Africa. "There's a wealth of VC funds established here, and B2B solutions tend to excel because of the strong business environment. Development is picking up pace."

[Apply to] joziangels.co.za

[Links] Web: joziangels.co.za LinkedIn: company/jozi-angels

- **Build a strong management team.**
  You should have a great founding team with a mix of
  innovative thinking, technology skills, operational skills,
  domain skills, selling skills and execution intelligence.

- **Prove your tech works.**
  Your technology should have a clearly defined
  competitive advantage that is unique, defensible
  and designed to scale at increasing profit margins.

- **Show traction.**
  We invest in post-revenue businesses with proof
  that customers want and will pay for the product.

- **Target an addressable market.**
  We want our portfolio companies to solve real
  problems in a growing market size.

- **Be tenacious.**
  The team needs a purpose, something that drives
  them to success and not money alone.

Kalon Venture Partners

[Name]

[Elevator Pitch]

"We invest in high-growth technology companies. We look for innovative business models that are geared to existing and emerging institutions and their customers."

[Sector]

Fintech

[Description]

Following a new trend in the South African space, Kalon Venture Partners is one of the better-known Section 12J venture capital funds, meaning any investors receive a 100 percent deduction on their taxable income as long as they stay invested for at least five years. Kalon uses its funds to back highly scalable tech startups and has invested in Flow, FinChatBot, i-Pay, SMEasy and Snapnsave. The fund was established by Clive Butkow on the back of his retirement from Accenture in 2012. "I wanted to follow my passion and purpose and help grow entrepreneurial businesses," he says. "In 2015, I noticed how disruptive technologies were taking off in South Africa and decided to start my own venture capital company."

Kalon Venture Partners focuses on providing disruptive digital technology startups with growth capital, with the goal of helping startups gain traction and positioning them for an ultimate exit of their businesses. The company sources its investments from a combination of events, networks and direct approaches, and it believes the Johannesburg space is a good one to be active in but sees room for improvement. "The Johannesburg startup scene is gaining traction, but I would like to see more coordinated initiatives between the multiple stakeholders and resources to help elevate it to that of the Western Cape," says Clive.

Kalon is a strategic investor where capital is the least important part of what it brings to the table, according to Clive. The company's mantra is to make heroes of the entrepreneurs. It does this through its board, which has over two hundred years of experience in venture capital and technology and domain expertise across various industries and business building skills. Kalon aims to be "the entrepreneurs behind the entrepreneurs." Besides capital, Kalon assists companies with strategy, operations, product design, sales, marketing and other business-building activities. "We provide mentorship capital to the founders to ensure they do not reinvent the wheel and leverage our extensive business-building experience."

[Apply to]

kalonvp.com/entrepreneur/apply-for-funding

[Links]

Web: **kalonvp.com** Facebook: **Kalonvp** Twitter: **@KalonVp** LinkedIn: **company/kalonvp**

directory

Startups

BrownSense Group
Spaces
Atrium on 5th Street
5th Street, Sandton
Johannesburg 2196
brownsensemarkets.co.za

Empty Trips
2 Merchant Place
1 Fredman Drive
Sandton
Johannesburg
emptytrips.com

FinChatBot
10 Van Beek Street
New Doornfontein
Johannesburg 2094
finchatbot.com

Fixxr
Tshimologong Precinct
41 Juta Street
Braamfontein
Johannesburg, 2001
fixxr.co.za

Homefarm
Media Mill, 07 Quince Street
Milpark, Johannesburg
myhomefarm.io

InvestSure
AlphaCode
1 Fredman Drive
Sandton
Johannesburg
investsure.info

Kenai
3rd Floor
2 Merchant Place
Cnr Rivonia Road and
Fredman Drive
Sandton
Johannesburg 2196
kenai.co.za

Raphta
4th Floor
73 Juta Street
Braamfontein
Johannesburg 2001
raphta.com

Syafunda
4th Floor Samro House
73 Juta Street
Braamfontein
Johannesburg 2001
syafunda.co.za

Tuta-me
9 Willow Brook Close
Melrose
Johannesburg 2196
tuta-me.com

Programs

AlphaCode
3rd Floor
2 Merchant Place
Cnr Fredman Drive
and Rivonia Road
Sandton
Johannesburg 2196
alphacodeincubate.club

Creative Enterprises Hub
J&B Hive
100 Juta Street
Braamfontein
Johannesburg 2000
creativeenterpriseshub.co.za

Endeavor
The Media Mill
Main Building, 2nd Floor
7 Quince Street
Milpark
Gauteng, 2092, South Africa
endeavor.co.za

The Innovation Hub
Mark Shuttleworth Street
Tshwane
theinnovationhub.com

JamLab (Journalism and Media Lab)
Journalism Department,
Wits University
10th Floor, University Building
c/n Jorissen & Bertha Streets
Braamfontein
Johannesburg 2000
jamlab.africa

The J&B Hive
J&B Hive
81 De Korte Street
Braamfontein
Johannesburg 2000
thejbhivejohannesburg.com

Raizcorp
Centex Close
Sandton 2196
raizcorp.com

Riversands Incubation Hub
8 Incubation Drive,
Riverside View Ext 15
Midrand
Johannesburg 2021
riversandsihub.co.za

Seed Engine
Building 2, 164 Katherine St
Barlow Park
Sandton, 2148
seedengine.co.za

Sw7
7 Spring Street
Rivonia
Sandton
Johannesburg 2128
sw7.co

Spaces

22 ON SLOANE
GEN Africa
22 Sloane Street
Bryanston, Sandton
Johannesburg 2191
22onsloane.co

AlphaCode
3rd Floor
2 Merchant Place
Cnr Fredman Drive
and Rivonia Road
Sandton
Johannesburg 2196
alphacode.club

Impact Hub Joburg
4th Floor East Wing
158 Jan Smuts Building
9 Walters Street
Rosebank
Johannesburg 2196
johannesburg.impacthub.net

The J&B Hive
J&B Hive
81 De Korte Street
Braamfontein
Johannesburg 2000
thejbhivejohannesburg.com

JoziHub
2nd Floor
44 Stanley Ave
Milpark
Johannesburg 2094
jozihub.org

Perch
37 Bath Ave
Rosebank
Johannesburg 2196
Perchoffices.co.za

**Tshimologong Digital
Innovation Precinct**
41 Juta Street, Braamfontein
Johannesburg 2001
tshimologong.joburg

Workshop17 West Street
138 West Street
Sandown
Sandton
Johannesburg 2031
workshop17.co.za/sandton

Experts

eKasiLabs
Innovation Centre
Mark Shuttleworth Street
Tshwane
theinnovationhub.com

Property Point
Workshop 17
138 West Street
Sandton
propertypoint.org.za

SAP South Africa (Pty.) Ltd.
SAP Business Park
1 Woodmead Drive
Woodmead
Johannesburg 2148
sap.com/africa

Founders

Bridge Labs
The Offices of Hyde Park
Block B, Strouthos Place
Hyde Park, Johannesburg 2196
bridgelabs.design

Rebeth Wines
Workshop 17
138 West Street
Sandton
2090
rebeth.co.za

RHTC Store
70 Juta Street
Johannesburg
rhtconline.wordpress.com

SiGNL
Cube Workspace Fourways
9 The Straight Avenue
Pineslopes
Fourways 2194
South Africa
Signl.co.za

Yococo
yococo.co.za

Schools

GIBS
26 Melville Road
Illovo
Sandton
Johannesburg 2196
gibs.co.za

**The University of
Johannesburg Centre for
Entrepreneurship (UJCfE)**
Johannesburg Business
School Towers
Cnr Barry Hertzog
& Napier Road
Milpark, Johannesburg 2092
uj.ac.za/faculties/cbe/ujcfe

WeThinkCode_
84 Albertina Sisulu Road
Johannesburg 2000
wethinkcode.co.za

Wits Business School
2 St David's Place
Parktown
Johannesburg 2050
wbs.ac.za

Investors

Edge Growth
Investment Place Office Park
1st Floor, Block B
10th Road
Off 2nd Avenue
Sandton
Johannesburg 2191
edgegrowth.com

Jozi Angels
1 Tana Road
Sunninghill
Sandton, 2157
joziangels.co.za

Kalon Venture Partners
71 Glenhove Square
4th Street, Houghton
Johannesburg 2198
kalonvp.com

Media Partner

Ventureburn
Burn Media Group
Cape Town | Johannesburg
| Brighton
ventureburn.com

Accountants

BDO
22 Wellington Road
Parktown
Johannesburg 2913
bdo.co.za/en-za

KPMG Wanooka Place
St. Andrews Road
Johannesburg 2193
kmpg.com

Massyns & Associates
7 Helston Street
New Redruth
Alberton
Johannesburg 1449
massyns-jhb.co.za

Moore Stephens
50 Oxford Road
Parktown
Johannesburg 2193
southafrica.moorestephens
.com

PwC
Waterfall City
4 Lisbon Lane
Jukskei View
Midrand
Johannesburg 2090
pwc.co.za

Banks

ABSA
absa.co.za

Capitec
capitecbank.co.za

Investec
investec.com

Nedbank
nedbank.co.za

Standard Bank
standardbank.co.za

Coffee Shops and Places with Wifi

Bean There Coffee
44 Stanley Ave
Milpark
Johannesburg 2092
beanthere.co.za

Cramers Coffee
17 Harrison Street
Johannesburg 2000
cramerscoffee.com

Father Coffee
73 Juta Street
Johannesburg 2000
fathercoffee.co.za

Motherland Coffee
189 Oxford Rd
Roseburg
Johannesburg 2196
motherlandcoffee.com

Starbucks Coffee Company
Tyrwhitt Ave & Cradock Ave
Rosebank
Johannesburg 2196
starbucks.co.za

Flats and Rentals

AA House
20 Wanderers Street
Johannesburg 2001
aa.co.za

Braamfontein Gate
209 Smit Street
Johannesburg 2001
braamfonteingate.co.za

Madison Lofts
26 Juta Street
Johannesburg 2000
property24.com

The Franklin
4 Pritchard Street
Johannesburg 2000
thefranklin.co.za

The Bolton, Rosebank
2 Sturdee Ave
Rosebank
Gauteng
Johannesburg 2196
thebolton.co.za

Urban Estate
53 2nd Road, Kew
Johannesburg 2090
urbanestate.co.za

Important Government Offices

Gauteng Department of Community Safety
64 Pritchard Street
Johannesburg 2000
gauteng.gov.za

Gauteng Department of Education
17 Simmonds Street
Johannesburg 2000
gauteng.gov.za

**Johannesburg Family
Court Centre**
1665 Albertina Sisulu Rd
Newtown
Johannesburg 2001
justice.gov.za

Johannesburg Post Office
Corner Jeppe & Small Street
Johannesburg 2000
postoffice.co.za

Master of The High Court
66 Marshalltown
Johannesburg 2107
justice.gov.za

Office of the Premier Gauteng
30 Simmonds Street
Marshalltown
Johannesburg 2107
provincialgovernment.co.za

Insurance Companies

AllLife
25 Ameshoff Street
Braamfontein
Johannesburg 2001
alllife.co.za

Hollard
81 Main Street
Marshalltown
Johannesburg 2000
hollard.co.za

Liberty
Liberty Life Centre
1 Ameshoff Street
Braamfontein
Johannesburg 2000
liberty.co.za

Old Mutual
107 Rivonia Rd, Sandown
Sandton
Johannesburg 2146
oldmutual.co.za

Safrican
195 Jan Smuts Ave
Johannesburg 2193
safrican.co.za

Santam Insurance
41 Stanley Ave
Braamfontein Werf
Johannesburg 2092
santam.co.za

Sanlam
3 Summit Rd, Morningside
Sandton
Johannesburg 2196
sanlam.co.za

Language Schools

Alliance Francaise
17 Lower Park Drive
Corner Kerry Road
Parkview
Johannesburg 2122
alliance.org.za

**Essential
English**
134 Grayston Drive
Sandton
Johannesburg 2196
essentailenglish.co.za

English Access
Louise Ave
Sandton
Johannesburg 2196
english.co.za

Language Lady
28 David Draper Rd
Bruma
Johannesburg 2198
languageladyca.za

**The Spanish Academy
South Africa**
161 6th Ave
Highlands North
Johannesburg 2192
spanishmadeeasy.co.za

Wits Language School
92 Empire Road
Parktown
Johannesburg 2193
witslanguageschool.com

Startup Events

AfricArena
africarena.co.za

Meetup.com Johannesburg
meetup.com/topics/entrepre-
neurship/za/johannesburg

**Southern Africa
Startup Awards**
southernafricastartupawards.
com

Seedstars Johannesburg
seedstars.com/cities/city/
Johannesburg

glossary

A

Accelerator
An organization or program that offers advice and resources to help small businesses grow

Acqui-hire
Buying out a company based on the skills of its staff rather than its service or product

Angel Investment
Outside funding with shared ownership equity

API
Application programming interface

ARR
Accounting (or average) rate of return: calculation generated from net income of the proposed capital investment

Artificial Intelligence
The simulation of human intelligence by computer systems; machines that are able to perform tasks normally carried out by humans

B

B2B
(Business-to-Business)
The exchange of services, information and/or products from a business to a business

B2C
(Business-to-Consumer)
The exchange of services, information and/or products from a business to a consumer

Blockchain
A digital, public collection of financial accounts in which transactions made in bitcoin or another cryptocurrency are recorded chronologically

BOM
(Bill of Materials)
A list of the parts or components required to build a product

Bootstrap
To self-fund, without outside investment

Bridge Loan
A loan taken out for a short-term period, typically between two weeks and three years, until long-term financing can be organized

Burn Rate
The amount of money a startup spends

Business Angel
An experienced entrepreneur or professional who provides starting or growth capital for promising startups

Business Model Canvas
A template that gives a coherent overview of the key drivers of a business in order to bring innovation into current or new business models

C

C-level
Chief position

Cap Table
An analysis of ownership stakes in a company

CMO
Chief marketing officer

Cold-Calling
The solicitation of potential customers who had no prior interaction with the solicitor

Convertible Note/Loan
A type of short-term debt often used by seed investors to delay establishing a valuation for the startup until a later round of funding or milestone

Coworking
A shared working environment

CPA
Cost per action

CPC
Cost per click

Cybersecurity
Technologies, processes and practices designed to protect against the criminal or unauthorized use of electronic data

D

Dealflow
Term for investors that refers to the rate at which they receive potential business deals

Deeptech
Companies founded on the discoveries or innovations of technologists and scientists

Diluting
A reduction in the ownership percentage of a share of stock due to new equity shares being issued

E

Elevator Pitch
A short summary used to quickly define a product or idea

Ethereum
A blockchain-based software platform and programming language that helps developers build and publish distributed applications

Exit
A way to transition the ownership of a company to another company

F

Fintech
Financial technology

Flex Desk
Shared desk in a space where coworkers are free to move around and sit wherever they like

I

Incubator
Facility established to nurture young startup firms during their first few months or years of development

Installed Base
The number of units of a certain type of product that have been sold and are actually being used

IP
(Intellectual Property) Property which is not tangible; the result of creativity, such as patents and copyrights

IPO
(Initial Public Offering) The first time a company's stock is offered for sale to the public

K

KPI
(Key Performance Indicator)
A value that is measurable and demonstrates how effectively a company is achieving key business objectives

L

Later-Stage
More mature startups/companies

Lean
Refers to 'lean startup methodology;' the method proposed by Eric Ries in his book for developing businesses and startups through product development cycles

Lean LaunchPad
A methodology for entrepreneurs to test and develop business models based on inquiring with and learning from customers

M

M&A
(Mergers and Acquisitions) A merger is when two companies join to form a new company, while an acquisition is the purchase of one company by another where no new company is formed

MAU
Monthly active user

MVP
Minimum viable product

O

Opportunities Fund
Investment in companies or sectors in areas where growth opportunities are anticipated

P

P2P
(Peer-to-Peer)
A network created when two or more PCs are connected and sharing resources without going through a separate server

Pitch Deck
A short version of a business plan presenting key figures generally to investors

PR-Kit (Press Kit)
Package of promotional materials, such as pictures, logos and descriptions of a company

Product-Market Fit
When a product has created significant customer value and its best target industries have been identified

Pro-market
A market economy/a capitalistic economy

S

SaaS
Software as a service

Scaleup
A company that has already validated its product in a market and is economically sustainable

Seed Funding
First round, small, early-stage investment from family members, friends, banks or an investor

Seed Investor
An investor focusing on the seed round

Seed Round
The first round of funding

Series A/B/C/D
The name of funding rounds that come after the seed stage

Shares
Units of ownership of a company that belong to a shareholder

Solopreneurs
A person who sets up and runs a business on their own and typically does not hire employees

Startup
Companies under three years old, in the growth stage and becoming profitable (if not already)

SVP
Senior Vice President

T

Term Sheet/Letter of Intent
The document between an investor and a startup including the conditions for financing (commonly non-binding)

U

Unicorn
A company often in the tech or software sector worth over US$1 billion

USP
Unique selling point

UX
(User experience design) The process of designing and improving user satisfaction with products so that they are useful, easy to use and pleasurable to interact with

V

VC
(Venture Capital) Financing from a pool of investors in a venture capital firm in return for equity

Vesting
Process that involves giving or earning a right to a present or future payment, benefit or asset

Z

Zebras
Companies which aim for sustainable prosperity and are powered by people who work together to create change beyond a positive financial return

Train Station - Johannesburg

STARTUP GUIDE *NORDICS*   The Entrepreneur's Handbook
STARTUP GUIDE *JOHANNESBURG*   The Entrepreneur's Handbook
STARTUP GUIDE *TRONDHEIM*   The Entrepreneur's Handbook
STARTUP GUIDE *HAMBURG*   The Entrepreneur's Handbook
STARTUP GUIDE *CAPE TOWN*   The Entrepreneur's Handbook
STARTUP GUIDE *LUXEMBOURG*   The Entrepreneur's Handbook
STARTUP GUIDE *VIENNA*   The Entrepreneur's Handbook
STARTUP GUIDE *TEL AVIV*   The Entrepreneur's Handbook
STARTUP GUIDE *MADRID*   The Entrepreneur's Handbook
STARTUP GUIDE *VALENCIA*   The Entrepreneur's Handbook
STARTUP GUIDE *COPENHAGEN*   The Entrepreneur's Handbook
STARTUP GUIDE *PARIS*   The Entrepreneur's Handbook
STARTUP GUIDE *REYKJAVIK*   The Entrepreneur's Handbook
STARTUP GUIDE *LOS ANGELES*   The Entrepreneur's Handbook
STARTUP GUIDE *STOCKHOLM*   The Entrepreneur's Handbook
STARTUP GUIDE *MUNICH*   The Entrepreneur's Handbook
STARTUP GUIDE *FRANKFURT*   The Entrepreneur's Handbook
STARTUP GUIDE *ZURICH*   The Entrepreneur's Handbook
STARTUP GUIDE *LONDON*   The Entrepreneur's Handbook
STARTUP GUIDE *LISBON*   The Entrepreneur's Handbook
STARTUP GUIDE *SINGAPORE*   The Entrepreneur's Handbook
STARTUP GUIDE *NEW YORK*   The Entrepreneur's Handbook
STARTUP GUIDE *BERLIN*   The Entrepreneur's Handbook
STARTUP GUIDE *OSLO*   The Entrepreneur's Handbook

→ startupguide.com   Follow us

About the Guide

Based on traditional guidebooks that can be carried around everywhere, Startup Guide books help you navigate and connect with different startup scenes across the globe. Each book is packed with useful information, exciting entrepreneur stories and insightful interviews with local experts. Today, Startup Guide books are in over two dozen cities in Europe, Asia, the US and the Middle East, including Berlin, London, Singapore, New York and Tel Aviv. As part of our partnership with One Tree Planted, each book we sell contributes toward the planting of a tree.

How we make the guides:

To ensure an accurate and trustworthy guide every time, we team up with local partners that are established in their respective startup scene. We then ask the local community to nominate startups, coworking spaces, founders, schools, investors, incubators and established businesses to be featured through an online submission form. Based on the results, these submissions are narrowed down to the top hundred organizations and individuals. Next, the local advisory board – which is selected by our community partners and consists of key players in the local startup community – votes for the final selection, ensuring a balanced representation of industries and startup stories in each book. The local community partners then work in close collaboration with our international editorial and design team to help research, organize interviews with journalists as well as plan photoshoots with photographers. Finally, all content is reviewed, edited and put into the book's layout by the Startup Guide team in Berlin and Lisbon before going for print in Berlin.

Where to find us: The easiest way to get your hands on a Startup Guide book is to order it from our online shop: startupguide.com/books

If you prefer to do things in real life, drop by one of the fine retailers listed on the stockists page on our website.

Want to become a stockist or suggest a store?

Get in touch here:
sales@startupguide.com

The Startup Guide Stores

Whether it's sniffing freshly printed books or holding an innovative product, we're huge fans of physical experiences. That's why we have stores in Berlin, Lisbon and Copenhagen. Not only do the stores showcase our books and a range of curated products, they're also our offices and a place for the community to come together and share wows and hows. But our stores wouldn't be possible without the help of Toyno, an experience design studio based in Lisbon. Visit their website here: toyno.com.

Lisbon:

Rua do Grilo 135, 1950-144 Lisboa, Portugal

Mon-Fri: 10h-18h

++351 21 139 8791

lisbon@startupguide.com

Berlin:

Maybachufer 6, 12047 Berlin, Germany

Mon-Fri: 10h-18h

+49 1 51 516 23 624

berlin@startupguide.com

Copenhagen:

Borgbjergsvej 1, 2450 Copenhagen, Denmark

Mon-Fri: 10h-16h

+45 52 17 85 45

copenhagen@startupguide.com

#startupeverywhere

Startup Guide was founded by Sissel Hansen in 2014. As a publishing and media company, we produce guidebooks and online content to help entrepreneurs navigate and connect with different startup scenes across the globe. As the world of work changes, our mission is to guide, empower and inspire people to start their own business anywhere. Today, Startup Guide books are in over two dozen cities in Europe, Asia, the US and the Middle East, including London, Stockholm, Vienna, Paris, Singapore, New York, Miami and Tel Aviv. We also have three physical stores in Berlin, Lisbon and Copenhagen which double as offices for our 20-person team.

Visit our website for more: startupguide.com

Want to get more info, be a partner or say hello?

Shoot us an email here: info@startupguide.com

Join us and #startupeverywhere

City Advisory Board

Andrea Warriner
African Management
Initiative
General Manager:
Southern Africa

Prof Barry Dwolatzky
JCSE at Wits University
Director

Kelebogile Molopyane
The Innovation Hub
Senior Manager: Maxum
Business Incubation

Kendal Makgamathe
Tshimologong Digital
Innovation Precinct
Events and Marketing
Manager

Kwena Mabotja
SAP
SAP Next-Gen Africa
Regional Director

Mike Stopforth
Beyond Binary
Director

Mixo Ngoveni
Geekulcha
Founder or CEO

Patrick Palmi
Justpalm.com
CEO

Shaun David Randles
TechNvst
Operations

Shawn Theunissen
Property Point and
Entrepreneurship
To The Point
Founder & CEO

Willem Gous
The Human
Entrepreneur
Founder

With thanks to our **Content Partners**

PROPERTYPOINT
A GROWTHPOINT INITIATIVE

Our **Ecosystem Partner**

And our **Media Supporters**

ventureburn
STARTUP NEWS FOR EMERGING MARKETS

With thanks to our **Community Partner**

UNIVERSITY OF THE
WITWATERSRAND,
JOHANNESBURG

TSHI
MOLO
GONG

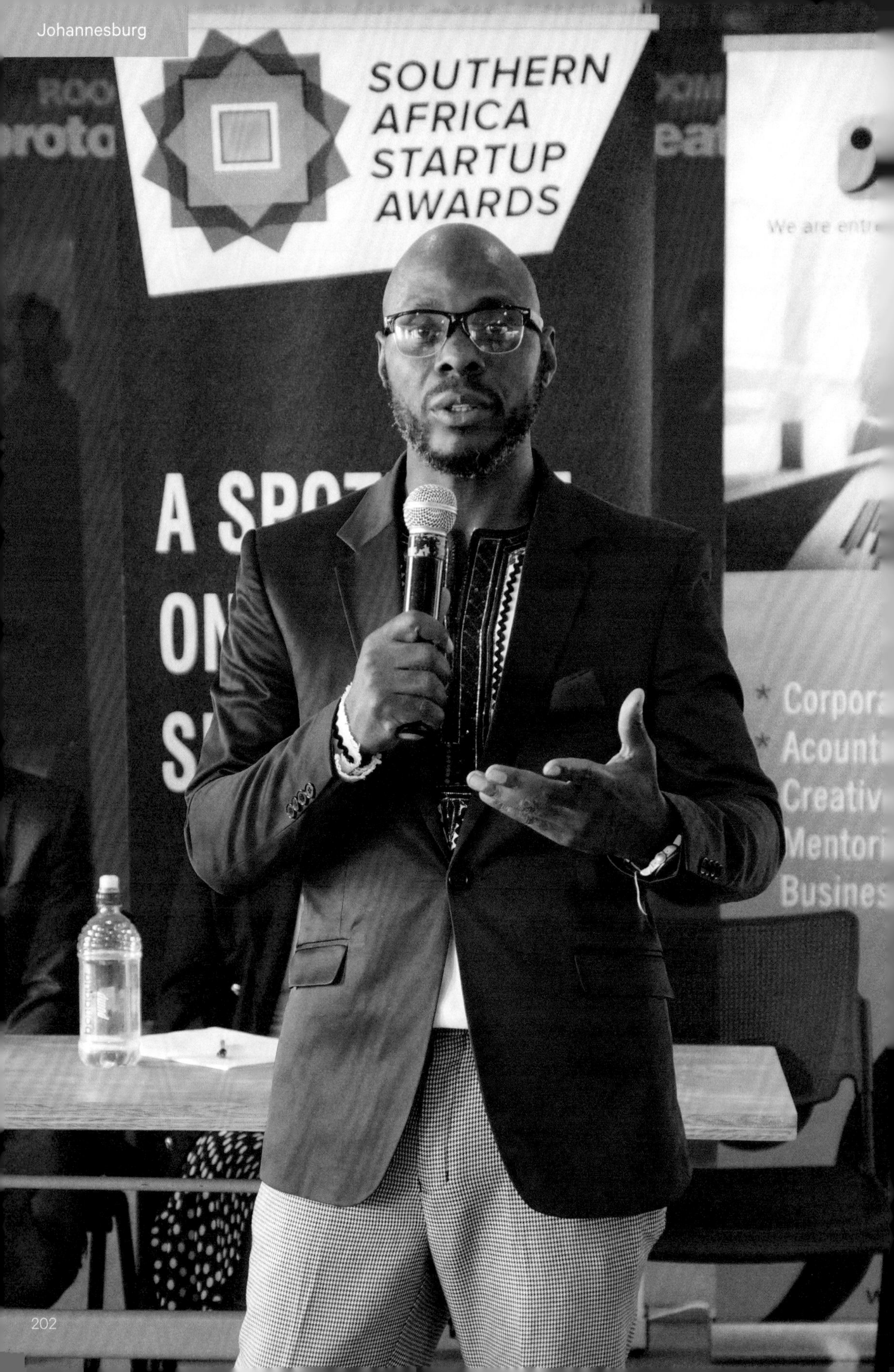
SOUTHERN
AFRICA
STARTUP
AWARDS

Ecosystem Partner / Southern Africa Startup Awards

[Summary] *"We enable, connect, support and celebrate key players in the national and regional startup ecosystems in Southern Africa for regional connectivity and global visibility, then fuse them together on a global entrepreneurial network, creating opportunities for international partnerships and commercial exchange."*

[Description] Southern Africa Startup Awards (SASAwards) is a registered nonprofit organization and a circuit of the Global Startup Awards (GSA). It is the first annual award to celebrate and recognize the spirit of innovation and achievement in the startup ecosystem in Southern Africa. GSA is a social enterprise that hosts annual events to award entrepreneurs within their respective tech/web industries who have shown outstanding achievements in business and service to the community and their regional startup ecosystems. It began as a way of recognizing entrepreneurs within the Nordic region and is now celebrated in sixty-four countries across seven regions, including the Nordics, South East Asia, Central Europe, SAARC Region (South Asia), East Asia, Baltics, and Southern Africa.

The Southern Africa Chapter, SASAwards, was founded in 2017 by Mckevin Ayaba, CEO of Setup A Startup, serial social entrepreneur, mentor and startup ecosystems builder, and one of the five winners of the inaugural 2015 Festival of Ideas competition organized by the Gordon Institute of Business Science. He has this to say: "We believe that startup ecosystems around the world play a crucial role in shaping our future for the better. Our mission is to find, enable, support and connect the top one percent from these global ecosystems."

In 2018, SASAwards launched its first edition. Over 3,200 nominations from fifteen countries were received in fifteen categories. National finalists were selected from each category to compete at the Regional Grand Finale. Thanks to our partnership with Limit Breakers Global Foundation, this took place at the amazing Steyn City, Johannesburg, and saw fifteen winners from fourteen countries walk away with prizes that included investment deals from Caban Investment Ltd, twelve months of free website development and services worth 150,000 ZAR each from Kaskade.Cloud.

Over and beyond the GSA objective, SASAwards hopes to weave a thread of unity and collaboration among African countries through entrepreneurship and innovation.

[Links] Web: **southernafricastartupawards.com** Facebook: **GSAwardsSouthernAfrica**

Editor of Ventureburn, Stephen Timm

Media Partner
/ Ventureburn

Ventureburn is a South Africa–based news and intelligence website founded in 2012 by the late Matthew Buckland, investor and entrepreneur. Now operating under the Burn Media Group umbrella, it focuses on technology startups, emerging businesses and the investor ecosystem across South Africa and the rest of Africa's hottest innovation hubs. *Ventureburn*, which is unashamedly independent, reports on critical news and analysis of the continent's tech startup scene.

The Burn Media Group also includes *Memeburn*, *Gearburn*, *Motorburn* and *Jobsburn*. Matthew Buckland was the former CEO and founder of Creative Spark, of which the Burn Media Group websites were a part. In June 2018, it was announced that the Burn Media Group had broken away from M&C Saatchi Abel's digital agency Creative Spark and had embarked upon a new "aggressive" growth curve. "There is an exciting entrepreneur and startup story developing in South Africa, Africa and the world," said Matthew at the time, "and we form part of the ecosystem as media to tell that story and accelerate the growth of the startup industry as a whole."

Led by General Manager Carl Davies and editor Stephen Timm, *Ventureburn* has emerged, in a short space of time, as the top startup and entrepreneur resource in the country and continent, with several new initiatives to be launched soon.

Visit **ventureburn.com** for more info.

Marshalltown - Johannesburg

WHERE NEXT?